SEVEN THINGS THEY DON'T TEACH YOU IN SEMINARY

OTHER BOOKS BY JOHN KILLINGER

Winter Soulstice: Celebrating the Spirituality of the Wisdom Years

The Devil & Harry Potter: A Christian Minister's Defense of the Beloved Novels
(St. Martin's, 2002)

Ten Things I Learned Wrong from a Conservative Church (Crossroad, 2002)

Lost in Wonder, Love, and Praise: Prayers and Affirmations for Christian Worship
(Abingdon, 2001)

Preaching the New Millennium (Abingdon, 1999)

Raising Your Spiritual Awareness Through 365 Simple Gifts from God
(Abingdon, 1998)

The Night Jessie Sang at the Opry (Angel Books, 1996)

*Preaching to a Church in Crisis: A Homiletic for the Last Days of the Mainline
Church* (CSS, 1996)

Day by Day with Jesus: A Devotional Commentary on the Four Gospels
(Abingdon, 1994)

Jessie: A Novel (McCracken, 1993)

Beginning Prayer (Upper Room, 1993)

Letting God Bless You: The Beatitudes for Today (Abingdon, 1992)

You Are What You Believe: The Apostles' Creed for Today (Abingdon, 1990)

Christmas Spoken Here (Broadman, 1989)

To My People with Love: The Ten Commandments for Today (Abingdon, 1988)

The God Named Hallowed: The Lord's Prayer for Today (Abingdon, 1987)

Christ and the Seasons of Marriage (Broadman, 1987)

Parables for Christmas (Abingdon, 1985)

Fundamentals of Preaching (Fortress, 1985; SCM, 1986; rev. 1998)

Christ in the Seasons of Ministry (Word, 1983)

The Loneliness of Children (Vanguard, 1980; Editions Robert Laffont, 1983)

His Power in You (Doubleday, 1978)

A Sense of His Presence (Doubleday, 1977)

Bread for the Wilderness, Wine for the Journey (Word, 1976)

The Salvation Tree (Harper & Row, 1973)

World in Collapse: The Vision of Absurd Drama (Dell, 1973)

The Fragile Presence: Transcendence in Contemporary Literature (Fortress, 1973)

Leave It to the Spirit: Freedom and Responsibility in the New Liturgies
(Harper & Row, 1971)

For God's Sake, Be Human (Word, 1970)

The Failure of Theology in Modern Literature (Abingdon, 1965)

Hemingway and the Dead Gods (University Press of Kentucky, 1960;
Citadel, 1965)

SEVEN THINGS THEY DON'T TEACH YOU IN SEMINARY

JOHN KILLINGER

A Crossroad Book
The Crossroad Publishing Company
New York

The Crossroad Publishing Company
16 Penn Plaza, Suite 1550,
New York, NY 10001

The text of this book is set in 11/16 Goudy Old Style
The display faces are Goudy Handtooled, Serio, Minion, and Nofret.

Printed in the United States of America

Library of Congress Cataloging-in-Publication Data is available
ISBN: 0-8245-2392-X

1   2   3   4   5   7   8   9   10   12   11   10   09   08   07   06

For all my former students,
with apologies
that I didn't teach you these things
when I was among you
– but, like most of your professors,
I simply didn't know them
then

Contents

A Word from the Author

I believe in the church. I really do. I don't believe, as one of the early church fathers said, that there is no salvation outside the church. That is entirely too narrow and parochial a viewpoint for the age in which we live. It is too proud and exclusivist, and unworthy of the God I worship, whose mercy is far more probing and wide-sweeping than the theologians of the church are willing to recognize. But I do believe in the church the way it is mentioned in the Apostles' Creed, as "the communion of saints." Saints, of course, are another matter. Some of them are saintly, as I imagine "saintly" ought to be, and others aren't. But in my own experience, there are few things better than the fellowship of sweet-spirited Christians.

Notice I said "sweet-spirited." That's bound to come up again later in the book.

I find it almost impossible to imagine what my life would have been like without the church. My father didn't attend church, and our home had almost no Christian overtones in it—no mention of God, no saying of grace at meals, no suggestion that our lives would be better if we were a church-going family instead of a basically secular one. But fortunately I was caught in one of the periodic sweeps of the ecclesiastical net that most churches in those days still called "revivals." I was eleven and had gone to Sunday school, not out of any religious compunction but because it was more pleasant than being at home with my father on a Sunday morning. The revival preacher made his obligatory pitch to the Sunday school classes. And bingo, he told a story that hit me right in my spiritual solar plexus, and I was "saved."

Nobody ever talked much about what it meant to be saved, beyond emphasizing that it meant one believed in Jesus and would be thereby rescued from the dangers of hellfire. There was no suggestion that one should grow in one's faith, or that one might even lose the small amount of it he or she had at that point of the pilgrimage. I was saved in a Baptist church, and Baptists taught "once saved, always saved," as distinguished from the Methodists, who the Baptist preacher always said were in error because they underestimated the divine persistence that never lets a saved person go.

From that time on, church became more or less everything to me and the church people became my real family. It's easy now to see how that happened. My home was a fractious place. My father and mother didn't get along because my father had a girlfriend in another town he went to see every Saturday afternoon, leaving my mother and me to clerk in their army-navy surplus store and close it up on Saturday night after the country folk had stopped coming in. Beside the tension in our house, the easy, cheerful camaraderie of the people in the church became a welcome refuge to me, and offered a kind of moral support without which my amounting to anything now seems almost unimaginable.

By the time I was fifteen, I already had a growing sense of destination in the ministry, although I tried to work out a compromise with God whereby I could become the magazine illustrator I wanted to be and serve him as a lay Christian and maybe even a Sunday school teacher. The final turn of the screw came when I was sixteen and went to a summer religious camp for a week of fellowship, fun, and serious worship. I'm not sure which of the three worked the greatest magic on me, but before the week had ended I had said yes to a calling to the ministry and did a complete U-turn in my plans to be an artist.

If the church had been supportive of me before that week, after that it was like the triumphal entry. I was hugged and congratulated, fêted and adored, by almost everybody in the congregation, from the youngest to the oldest, and the minister, a strong, scholarly man who walked the streets so erectly that I sometimes wondered if he had a shovel handle for a spine, practically adopted me as a son. From then on I was always welcome in his home, even on Sunday afternoons when he was prone to take a nap, and we had long discussions about college and seminary and all the things I needed to be thinking about now that I myself was going to be a minister.

⌒

I sometimes wonder what my life would have been like if I had become an artist instead of a minister. In those days almost everybody read *Life*, *Look*, *Collier's*, and The *Saturday Evening Post*. They were as ubiquitous as *Us*, *People*, and *Entertainment* are today. I was partial to the *Saturday Evening Post* because it had covers painted by Norman Rockwell and other artists and inside it had a lot of funny cartoons. I could envision myself as the next Norman Rockwell. There wasn't anything I couldn't draw or paint, and everybody said they were amazed at the talent I had. When I was fifteen, I sent off more than two hundred dollars—half of everything I had saved for college—for tuition in the Famous Artists' School, a mail-order course in illustrating supposedly sponsored by Rockwell and other *Saturday Evening Post* artists. I was disappointed when I did the required homework and never saw any evidence that Rockwell or any other artist whose name I recognized ever laid eyes on anything I drew or painted. But the exercises in the course were helpful, and I still imagined myself as Rockwell's successor.

It was also part of my adolescent dream to own some land in the Bluegrass area of Kentucky. We lived in Somerset, eighty miles south of Lexington, the heart of the Bluegrass. I loved the out-of-doors, and liked to picture myself living in a house on a few acres of that beautifully rolling land around Lexington, working at my easel until I got tired, then strolling outside among grazing horses and a couple of happy, boisterous dogs. I would have a beautiful wife, of course, and we would belong to a church in Lexington, and I might even become a Sunday school teacher there if my busy career as an artist would permit it.

I am vain enough to think that I might have made this beautiful dream come true, at least in its external outlines. One of my acquaintances at Somerset High School, a sleepy-eyed boy named Malcolm Greer, who was two years older than I, went on to Cincinnati Art School and became one of the most prominent designers in the East, teaching at Brown University and managing a prestigious art firm in that area. Among his claims to fame are the designs of the logo of the Presbyterian Church, U.S.A., a postage stamp for the U.S. government, and the interior environment of Somerset's community college. I've always thought that if Malcolm could achieve so much, there wasn't any reason that I couldn't achieve my ambitions as well, especially as they were apparently more modest than his.

But what would my life have been like along with that dream? Most magazines stopped using illustrators a few years after that. Even the *Saturday Evening Post,* when it was revived after a few years' hiatus, didn't strive for the same artistic look it had once had. When computers came in, the art departments of most journals and newspapers went almost entirely to technological design. One of my sons became a professional artist, and found that he had only two sure ways of earning a living: working as a graphic designer for a printing company or teaching school. I would have hit that crunch at some point in my career, even if I had had a few years of doing it Norman Rockwell's way.

I might have belonged to a church and continued to enjoy the fellowship of some kindred spirits within it. But I would also have become involved in the politics of a congregation, and might well, as some of my friends have done through the years, have walked away from it in disgust.

As it is, I have been involved with the church almost all of my life. I have had many a lover's quarrel with it, but it has always remained important to me and I have never—except perhaps in recent days— wanted to walk away from it. I have continued to see it as "the length- ened shadow of one man," as Emerson put it, and have never lost my attraction for the Christ who continues to cast that giant shadow. There is never a day when he is not somehow mystically at the center of it, challenging my thinking, stimulating my imagination, and commanding my loyalty and admiration.

≺⌐

Most of the tension I have experienced in the church—in the *seven* churches I have pastored—has arisen from the struggle between Christ and his church, or at least between the Christ of my imagination and the church as I have known it. If I had not been so committed to the One who "saved" me back there when I was a youngster in Sunday school, and so insistent on learning more about him and what his teaching and example mean for life today, I would have had a much easier time as a minister. But we shall get into that presently, and I need not explain it further at this point.

I said I have pastored seven churches. I like that, because I am partial to Hebrew numerology. Seven is a very biblical number. Two of the churches—my first two—were essentially rural parishes, one at Bronston, Kentucky, and the other in a little community called Willaila, in Rockcastle County, Kentucky. With the exception of a few nurses, teachers, and office workers, the members were all farmers and farmers' wives. They were good people—the salt of the earth. I have never forgotten their kindness and generosity toward a young, ignorant preacher who came among them on weekends from his Mt. Olympus at the university and shared his passions with them in exchange for a lot of Sunday dinners and the minuscule salaries that went with the territory.

My third church, also a student parish, was Martin's Pond Union Baptist Church in North Reading, Massachusetts, a northern suburb of Boston and Cambridge, where I was attending divinity school at Harvard University. Most of our congregants there were salespeople, teachers, mechanics, construction workers, clerks, and blue-collar workers in the Boston metroplex. In a sense, they were better educated than most of our previous church members. Even those who had not been to college read the Boston *Globe*, worked among well-educated people, and knew what was transpiring in the world around them. But because the church was small and struggling, there was a sense of joy and unity in the little congregation much like that I'd known in my previous churches, and my wife and I enjoyed being there so much that it was very hard to leave.

Because I was a Baptist at this stage of my journey, and most Baptists (especially Southern Baptists from whom I'd sprung) were suspicious of "too much education," I found it very difficult to locate in a congregation whose size and program were commensurate with my training. So I ended up becoming a teacher for a few years, first at Georgetown College in Kentucky, then at Princeton, where I took a second doctor's degree, then at Kentucky Southern College in Louisville, where I was the academic dean, and eventually at Vanderbilt Divinity School in Nashville, where for fifteen years I enjoyed an almost idyllic life of teaching, traveling, and writing. Finally, at mid-life, when the psychologists say we often want to go back and reclaim a part of our journey we have neglected until then, I felt an overwhelming desire to return to the pastorate, and this time, forsaking the Baptists (who had essentially forsaken me), moved to a large congregation.

My fourth parish experience came while I was technically still employed by Georgetown College and went off to Princeton Seminary for a couple of years to study with one of my ministerial idols, a Lutheran pastor named Paul E. Scherer. While I was at Princeton, I became the minister of a small Baptist chapel in Metuchen, New Jersey, halfway between Princeton and New York. The chapel was part of Southern Baptists' "homeland missions" program, which had an emphasis on founding new churches in major metropolitan areas like New York, Chicago, and Boston. It had been in existence for a few months when I arrived, but I was its first regular pastor.

The congregation had no church building, but rented a public school building in Metuchen for Sunday school and worship services. Members kept the folding cribs, playpens, and other paraphernalia for a nursery in their homes, as well as hymnals and Sunday school materials, and transported them to Sunday meetings in the backs of their cars and station wagons. My responsibilities included leading the worship and preaching, calling on the sick, visiting an occasional shut-in, and counseling anyone who sought the pastor's help. Like my previous churches, this was essentially a weekend charge.

The congregants in this church were a varied lot, and many of them were very alert, creative people. One man, Wayne McCann, was manager of a large overseas petroleum organization, and spent a lot of time flying to Europe and the Middle East. Another, Dean McAdoo, was a young engineer with Noise, Unlimited, an acoustics company that worked for Boeing Aircraft, and he and a partner named Dick Strange bought out their company and Dean eventually developed it into one of the largest acoustics firms in the country. A man named Jim Lane was a pilot for Eastern Airlines, and flew the New York-Miami route on a regular basis. James McClenney was a transportation director for Coca-Cola Company, and subsequently moved to Orlando as vice president of Coca-Cola and Minute Maid in charge of all their transportation. Most of these people and the others in the church were about the same age, in their thirties and forties, and our fellowship was warm and exciting. And the fact that we were only starting a church, and had no traditions from the past to govern our actions, made it a very heady and challenging experience for all of us.

My fifth tenure as a pastor, when I left Vanderbilt Divinity School, was at the First Presbyterian Church (FPC) of Lynchburg, Virginia, an old, dignified, yet very active congregation in a city of 75,000 people where Jerry Falwell was the favorite son. FPC Lynchburg was the kind of church most ministers come to when they've done their yeoman's work in moderate-sized churches elsewhere. I had pastored four small churches and then had the leisurely life of a professor for twenty years. Within a few days of immersing myself in this new church, I felt like a diver getting the bends. The water was deeper than I imagined. I think it was while I was in Lynchburg and giving some lectures at the summer Pastor's Institute at Princeton Theological Seminary that I said I felt as if I had fallen into a pool full of piranhas and there was soon little left of me but a stain in the water!

FPC Lynchburg was a strong church, with lots of warmth and plenty of muscle. There were sixty-five medical doctors in the congregation, and probably an equal number of lawyers and teachers. Many of the members were world travelers. George Stewart, who was president of First Colony Life Insurance and probably the wealthiest man in town, was an avid Bible student and taught a popular men's Sunday school class. The church was literally oozing with clout, talent, and enthusiasm.

From there I went to my sixth church, the First Congregational Church of Los Angeles, the oldest English-speaking congregation in the City of Angels. It was sold to me as a big, powerful institution, certainly one of the most prestigious churches in that sprawling metropolis. There we hobnobbed with actors, artists, and musicians as well as doctors, lawyers, teachers, and CEOs. As it turned out — nobody had bothered to count lately — the congregation was a lot smaller than anybody thought (that's a story for later), but it was certainly diverse, interesting, and demanding. I had been there less than a month when I came home from a council meeting one night and said to my wife, Anne, "This isn't what we thought it was, and I don't want to stay. But let's not leave until after the first of the year, so it won't look as bad on my résumè." More than once I would write in my diary, "If I don't get out of here soon, it's going to kill me." We stayed three years, and when I left I wasn't interested in another church. I became a professor of religion and culture at Samford University in Birmingham, Alabama.

My seventh church wasn't actually a full-time church. It was the Little Stone Church on Mackinac Island, Michigan, a choice little resort church in a community that thrived in the summers and then almost ceased to exist in the winters. I was minister of this unusual congregation for eight years. We lived at home (Birmingham, then Williamsburg,

Virginia, and finally Warrenton, Virginia) seven and a half months each year and went to the church for four and a half months. It was an annual ritual of packing up our station wagon in May, moving to the island, loading up again in October, and heading for home. Talk about human yoyos! But it was an interesting experience in several ways. First, there was the fascinating culture of the island itself, which was mostly Roman Catholic and basically anticultural. Then there was the congregation, which numbered about fifty when we went there and a hundred when we left, and included a greater percentage of wealthy people than any church I ever pastored. Few of them lived on the island year-round. Most had two and even three or four homes, including at least one in Florida. And finally there were the visitors—the real heartbeat of everything—who arrived by the droves in the summer from all points of the globe. Many returned to the Little Stone Church every time they came to the island, and brought a freshness with them unlike any on the island itself.

Seven churches, like the seven churches of the book of Revelation. I've never tried to match them up with those biblical churches, to see which one was neither hot nor cold, which one pretentiously rich, etc. But like some of the churches in Revelation, I'm sure there was something wrong with each one of them. Maybe a lot of somethings. I didn't expect this back when I was young. Nobody told me that congregations can be mean or grudging or spiteful. Nobody told me that churches can be their own worst enemies, and interfere with the flow of divine spirit almost as a matter of course.

～

On the whole, it is my opinion that smaller churches are kinder and less dangerous places to be than large ones. There is generally more unanimity in them and less agitation for this cause or that. And in country churches particularly there are simpler people who are more in touch with themselves and therefore more likely to be tolerant and forgiving. People who live close to the land are less prone to be conspiratorial and mean-spirited than people in cities.

I remember a Disciples of Christ minister I met several years ago when I was speaking at a preaching conference in Jefferson City, Missouri. He struck me as one of the few ministers there who were obviously happy with their parishes. When I commented on this, he said, "Oh, I've got good reason to be happy. I recently left a church of fifteen hundred members to become the minister of a congregation of a hundred and fifty. The difference is like night and day. Now I can take off almost any time I want to and go fishing. I love to fish. But if anybody in my last church heard that the minister had gone fishing, they'd say, 'We're not paying him to go fishing. He ought to be in his office!'"

None of my professors in seminary ever warned me about big churches. In fact, none of them ever warned me about a single thing. They were smart and eloquent, and they knew a lot about a lot of subjects, everything from Ugaritic to patristics, and atonement theories to arguments for and against the afterlife. But most of them, I've realized since, were teaching in seminary because (a) they couldn't get a church or (b) they couldn't stand the life of the ministry and so had retreated to professorial positions. I could count on the fingers of one hand all the really successful ministers I ever had a chance to learn from, and they, because they were too proud to admit it or knew better than to discourage the troops, weren't talking.

Consequently, there were several hard lessons I had to learn on the job, as it were, things that were often discouraging and sometimes all but destructive. That's the stuff of this book—seven things that should have been taught in seminary but weren't because the professors either didn't know them from experience or weren't willing to impart them for fear of repelling us would-be ministers before we got to the front lines. Frankly, I wish somebody had taught them to me—had spelled them out in all their burden and horror so that I would have known what I was getting into and wouldn't have felt so many times as if I and I alone had faced such torments and that I was therefore guilty of doing everything wrong and bringing about my own downfall. There is a lot to be said for forewarning. Future doctors are warned in medical school about things that can go wrong in the operating room, and about patients who are likely to bring legal action against them for mistakes they make under fire. Budding lawyers are warned about people who will lie under oath and about tricks their opponents will almost surely play in the courtroom. Even teachers are warned that some students are rebellious and others are simply unteachable, and are given tactics to employ when they encounter such pupils. But it's almost as if there's a conspiracy not to tell future ministers what they are getting into because, if it were told, then the church wouldn't be the glorious entity it is and we would all be aware of its failings and injustices.

࿎

Perhaps I shouldn't be writing this book. Why perpetuate the faults of the church by talking about them? Some readers will be angry with me for having said the things I intend to say. They will call me a malcontent and a troublemaker, and suggest that I encountered the problems I write about because I was simply not good enough or wasn't looking at my difficulties through the right devotional prism. One thing I've learned after years in the ministry is that there are two sides to almost everything and some people will find them even if they have the same face on them. And because I've learned this I've also learned not to worry very much about what the dissidents say. They wouldn't be happy if they didn't have something to fuss about.

Maybe I wouldn't either. Which is to say, I'm not self-righteous about it. I just write about what I see and feel, and if people don't like it, well, I'm sorry they feel that way but it's a free country, or at least I think it still is, and being able to express yourself is what that's all about.

But I can promise the reader, especially if you are considering going into the Christian ministry, that the things in this book are true and someday they will matter to you in ways that you cannot presently know or predict. So don't read this book and then sell it or throw it away. Put it on the shelf by your Bible and a few other books you see regularly and keep it there until the day comes when you want to pick it up and read something in it again. For you will, because the things I'm talking about in this book are going to pop up in your own consciousness before you're ready for them to, and then this book will be a comfort to you, not because it has any good answers for all the things it talks about but because it is always helpful, when we are going through a bad patch in life, to realize that somebody else has been miserable before us, and in almost precisely the same way. Then you will take down this book, find the passage that is most relevant at the time, and kiss it because it will make you feel better not to be the only minister who's ever been through the problem it talks about.

One

Churches Are Really Institutions, Not Centers of Spirituality

I'm a very slow learner. There were a lot of things I should have known about churches from having belonged to several, but I didn't. After two tall-steeple experiences, I had to go back to teaching in order to reflect on what I had seen and learned, and then I was amazed at the simple insight that came to me. I chided myself for being fifty-six years old and not having seen it before: *Most large churches aren't really part of a dedicated Christian movement, they are only secular institutions.* They may have been devoted to Christ in the beginning, and eagerly sought the leadership of God's Spirit. But in the course of the years, they gradually turned into something else—major organizations that function mainly along the lines of other organizations such as schools and banks and insurance companies.

The worst part of this, of course, is that something very crucial is missing right at the heart of the church. The Spirit has gone AWOL in favor of machinery and functionality. The very genius of Christianity, the sense of what we are about, has disappeared, and in its place there stands a big building with all the evidences of its being a church: a spire or a tower, a sanctuary, a pulpit and a table, classrooms and offices, copy machines, a telephone system, and usually a kitchen and a dining area. It is an indictment of our spirituality that we think of these appurtenances as constituting a church, for they don't. A real church is something else altogether, and it can exist in a cave, a house, or a motel room. I once knew a church that met in a bar, and I have known a number that met in schools. But we have let ourselves be blinded by the traditional paraphernalia and think we are seeing a church when we aren't!

I give the credit for this remarkable insight—it is really much more profound than it first appears—to Lyle Schaller, the business pro turned church guru, who mentioned in a book called *It's a Different World!* that churches go through an evolutionary pattern similar to that discernible in businesses. There is an incandescent stage when they first appear, then a growing and cooling period in which they begin to get organized, and finally a management stage in which they work at developing their assets and capitalizing their advantages. A business is usually initiated by some passionate entrepreneur who operates it out of a home, basement, or small shop, then moves it to larger quarters and employs more people as it develops. In its middle stage, it is exciting and nourishing to all its participants because they can see things really beginning to happen. But eventually it grows into a large, impersonal kind of company where everything is done by MBA procedures and people are rewarded for playing by the rules, not for having a spirit of innovation and exploration.

As I thought about it, I realized that the most important shift that occurs between a newly launched business and one that has moved through the stages to incorporation is one from an ad-hoc status where ingenuity and spirit are rewarded to a more rigidly programmed existence where ingenuity and spirit are muscled aside by simple bottom-line budgetary results. Big companies such as Merck and G.E. and Chrysler may proclaim to the public that they are driven by spirit, but the plain, unavoidable fact is that they are ultimately governed by budget and budget alone.

"Holy church towers!" I thought as the truth of this insight began to dawn on me. "This is precisely the way it was at the First Congregational Church of Los Angeles!"

⌒

FCC/LA was one of the most impressive churches I have ever known. It had had an impressive array of great ministers. One of these, in the 1920s, was Lloyd C. Douglas, who would later become famous as the author of *Magnificent Obsession, The Robe, The Big Fisherman,* and other popular religious novels. Douglas didn't like First Congregational Church. It had already become too much of a corporation for his spiritual taste. He thought there were too many bosses among the high-powered laypeople. One day when he had just returned from visiting his daughters in France, where they were going to school, one of these laymen laid certain demands on his desk about the way he was to manage the church's financial campaign. The next Sunday Douglas got into the pulpit and read his resignation. He did not wish to be part of such a spiritless, budget-minded institution, he said. His ministry in L.A. had lasted a little over two years. When the church later published a handsome book called *Light on a Gothic Tower* as part of its centenary celebration, the chapter about Douglas was entitled "The Douglas Interlude."

In 1932, the church moved from its old quarters at Ninth and Hope in Central Los Angeles to a glorious new sanctuary at Sixth and Commonwealth, on the edge of the city where it was still surrounded by orange groves. The architects of this new building had scoured England and Europe for models, and had constructed the church tower, which is visible for more than a mile to drivers approaching from downtown by Sixth Avenue, on the model of the one at Magdalen College, Oxford. But it was still in the Depression era, and the church soon found itself unable to pay off its mortgage, which for those days was quite large—$75,000. So in 1935, it turned to a minister in Grand Rapids, Michigan, who was noted for his fund-raising abilities. During the Depression era when most ministers were lucky to be able to put bread and potatoes on the table, Dr. James W. Fifield, Jr., was raking in $150,000 a year with a popular radio program.

Fifield liked FCC's new building and liked the idea of being a minister on the edge of Hollywood. The very location seemed to give more scope to his grandiose personality. He would come, he said, but only if the church fathers agreed to his having strict control of everything in the church. They knew that such a demand flew in the face of all their Congregational polity, but they were so desperate that they said OK.

Even a spiritualist like myself has to admire Fifield's style. The first thing he did when he got to L.A. was to set up a conference at the bank with all its directors. "We shall pay you the $75,000 we owe you," he said. "Every cent of it. But first I need to borrow another one million dollars." We can only imagine how astonished the bank directors were at this new minister's brash self-confidence, for none of the details of the pursuant discussion have survived. But at the end of an hour's conference, Fifield walked out of the meeting with an additional million dollars of credit.

Like the head of a new government agency in Washington, he began hiring the people he needed to make First Congregational Church a thriving concern. Soon there were several new ministers on the staff. He bought a limousine and hired a chauffeur to take him around town to all the meetings he was going to attend and all the homes where he was going to call. He joined the famous—and notoriously expensive—Jonathan Club, the most exclusive men's club in the city. He built himself a new house a mile or so from the church, a mansion that he eventually sold to Mohammed Ali, the heavyweight boxing champion. He obviously knew that in order to attract money you have to look like money. He had the business-savvy mind of a CEO and a financier.

Fifield paid off First Church's debt in less than seven years, and went on to build significant new additions to the already stately church. He charmed Mrs. Frank Roger Seaver, a wealthy benefactress who later contributed a beautiful theater to Pepperdine University, into giving the money to build Pilgrim School, a K-12 institution for four hundred gifted children of all races. Mrs. Seaver was still living when I became the senior minister at First Congregational Church and one of the first obligations laid upon me was to call on her. The church's financial secretary, Mrs. Nannette Coggins, who had been there since Fifield's time and knew all the great benefactors, set up the meeting. I was admitted to Mrs. Seaver's home by a nurse. I sat alone in the parlor for several minutes while she was prepared for our meeting. She was quite elderly by then and appeared in a wheel chair. She was pleasant and I am sure I fawned over her appropriately, but it was obvious that she was no longer either physically or mentally strong. I felt sad as I left the house because I could sense what a strong and attractive woman she had once been.

Fifield ruled First Congregational Church for thirty-two years. He was a tall, slender man, and liked being known as "the tall preacher." In fact, that was the name he gave to his autobiography. He made friends with all the wealthy and the famous in Los Angeles. He had an Easter Eve Vigil service crafted for none other than Charlton Heston, who became a member of the church and for several years read the dramatic parts of the service every Easter Eve. Ronald Reagan emceed a program at the church. During the time of the anticommunist movement in America, Fifield started the church's Freedom Club, and had important national speakers including Senator Barry Goldwater and Senator Joseph McCarthy to address the great crowds it drew. While the church was very liberal in its theology, it became extremely conservative in its membership.

The large desk in Fifield's office sat on a dais so that people who came to see him sat several inches lower than he did. When I learned about this, I thought of Charles de Gaulle, also a tall man, who did the same thing at the Élysées palace in Paris. Anne and I had once seen de Gaulle passing in his limousine as we waited on a streetlight near the Place d'Alma, not far from the American Church where we were living. It was dark, and he was sitting high in the back seat of the limousine with a little spotlight focused on him so that people on the street could see who was passing.

A friend of mine and my associate minister at First Congregational Church, Dr. Walter J. Vernon, recalls that when he was a young minister in Anaheim, he saw Fifield while he himself was waiting at a stoplight in his Volkswagen Beetle. Dr. Fifield's limousine, driven by a chauffeur, pulled up beside him and Fifield gave him a little waving gesture. It's a vignette Walt has never forgotten.

When Fifield finally retired from the ministry in 1967, he left an enormous power vacuum at the heart of the church. A number of significant persons rushed to fill that vacuum, including several attorneys on the major boards of the church. The ministers who followed Fifield suffered greatly at the hands of these power-mongers. One had a nervous breakdown. Another reported that when he left the church, they followed him for years with malicious intent to destroy his life and ministry. The ghost of Fifield lived on, exerting a kind of sinister effect on the life of the congregation.

Once, while I was minister at the church, my wife had lunch with Dr. Marion Luenberger, a former moderator of the church who had also been moderator of the National Association of Congregational Christian Churches. They had enjoyed shrimp salad at Bullock's-Wilshire, a lovely, upscale department store a few blocks from the church, and it had been heavily laced with garlic. On their way back to the church, where Dr. Luenberger had a meeting, she suggested that they chew some gum to mitigate the garlic odor on their breath. As they stood and chatted a minute more beneath a large tree in the church's courtyard, Anne absent-mindedly plucked a leaf from the tree and was twirling it between her fingers. Dr. Luenberger's face became instantly contorted. "You've pulled a leaf off the James Fifield tree!" she exclaimed. It was one of two large, handsome ficuses, one of which bore a dedicatory plaque to Fifield and another to his brother. Without missing a beat in what she was saying, Anne took the gum out of her mouth, made a little wad of it around the stem of the leaf, and fastened it to a branch of the tree. "There," she said airily, and went on talking.

We have laughed about that incident several times, but I relate it here because it illustrates how the tall shadow of Fifield lay across the life and work of First Congregational Church long after he was gone. Had he been a great saint, a Savonarola or a Mother Teresa, that would have been fine. His spirit would have continued to bless and heal people long after he had left. But because he was a virtual tyrant who had shaped everything around himself and his own hunger for power, his lingering influence was baleful and destructive.

Dr. Jack Hayford, the well-known pastor of the Church on the Way in San Fernando, California, told me once that he and his wife were driving past First Congregational Church on their way to a dinner in downtown L.A. when he felt a strange aura around the church. He circled the block, trying to discern what it was. "Jack," said his wife, "we're going to be late. What are you doing?" "In a minute," he said. "I'm trying to figure this out. God is hurting in this church. I can feel it from here." I have a lot of respect for Jack. If he thought he felt God hurting in First Congregational Church, he was probably right.

Fifield was a CEO, not a true Christian pastor. That's the long and short of it. And because he was such a powerful CEO, holding the reins to everything so tightly to himself, he left an ugly mark on the church for all time to come. The church was very "successful" under his reign. It attracted the rich and famous, and had a lot of influence in the city. It became the largest Congregational church in the world, and carried a lot of weight in the denomination. Its church plant expanded to cover several city blocks, and in addition it acquired a cemetery, two apartment buildings, and a beautiful 270-acre campground at Big Bear, in the mountains east of L.A., where many famous movies were filmed as well as most of the *Lassie, Bonanza, and Sergeant Preston of the Yukon* television series. That property is, of course, now priceless.

But African-Americans have told me that when they attempted to join First Congregational Church Fifield would get them aside and try to persuade them that there were other churches where they'd be much happier, because he wanted to maintain an image of elitism and white supremacy in his congregation. And he was far more interested in belonging to the Jonathan Club and other exclusive organizations, and in attracting nationally known speakers to his own Freedom Club, than he was in ministering to the growing number of poor and homeless people in the city. He was a great institution-builder but he was not much of a Christian pastor.

The moment I realized that most old churches are institutions in themselves and not necessarily part of the Christian movement, I knew why I had never really felt comfortable as the minister of the First Congregational Church of Los Angeles. I had become a minister to be part of Christ's growing kingdom, not to preside over an institution that had long ago ceased to care about the kingdom. I had a passion for the gospel, a passion for the poor, a passion for loving. The church didn't have a passion for anything except preserving its heritage. I preached Sunday after Sunday on the love of God and the difference it can make in the world; and then I went to board and committee meetings and listened to arguments and harangues that made me wonder if people had heard a word I was saying. I comported myself as a pastor and a gentleman at all times, and couldn't understand why some of our members were as antagonistic to me as if I were Old Scratch himself. And it didn't matter how hard I worked or how earnestly I prayed, I didn't seem to be able to budge that old church along one inch toward the kingdom of God. It was as reprobate and unredeemed when I left as it had been when I came.

I stayed three years at First Church, a little longer than Lloyd C. Douglas had stayed. But when I left, I did so because I realized that my vision of Christianity and the church's were so far apart that I didn't have enough years left to change it. The powerful old laymen in the church (and a few of the laywomen too) wanted the church to recapture the glory of its past, in the heyday of Fifield and the Freedom Club. I looked around us and saw thousands of immigrants pouring into our neighborhood every week and needing every kind of assistance human beings can require, and I said we ought to become a feeding station for the poor and a housing agency for the homeless. In fact, I believed that God wanted all of us big old churches in the mid-Wilshire area to pool our resources, sell some of our valuable property, build a hotel for homeless families and a cafeteria for the poor, and join hands to eliminate illiteracy, violent gang life, and drug dependency in our part of the city. But I had learned enough about the institution I pastored to realize that none of those dying churches was going to trust God enough to cede an inch of their property or reach out to God's little ones, and like towns that had lost their highways or railroads, they were going to wither and die within the next two or three decades.

Some of the church leaders accused me of not having any vision. They meant that I couldn't see what they thought they could see, a renewal of that old Caucasian church as an institution of power and influence at Sixth and Commonwealth, marooned in a sea of black, brown, and yellow faces but sailing right along on the breeze from a big PR budget and a series of famous organ concerts that attracted musicians from all over L.A. A big-time attorney who idolized Fifield and headed an office of more than 250 attorneys, arrived drunk at a gala evening to raise money for our annual Los Angeles Bach Festival and spent more than an hour excoriating me as a disappointment and a quitter because I had said in a recent Pentecost sermon that the most spiritual thing we could do as a church might be to deed our property to one of the fast-growing Korean churches in the area and say, "Here, it's yours. We've had it a long time, and now God wants you to use it."

☙

Even after I discovered the truth about the institutional church, I liked to think that the Baptist church I grew up in was different. There was a strong emphasis in that church on Christ and evangelism. (The fact that the Christ who was preached was the Christ of evangelism, the one who had died for the sins of the world, and not the Christ of radical social ideas, is also important, but perhaps not relevant here.) Diurnal revivalism—a spring revival and a fall revival—were a fact of life in its culture. Surely that mitigated the development of a real institutionalism in the congregation.

Who was I kidding?

As I pondered the matter, I realized that the formidable old group of church fathers, the deacons and trustees, were never converted in the revivals. The preachers always pled with backsliding Christians to "get right with God" again and register their renewal by coming forward with the people who were confessing Christ as their Savior. This call was usually answered by two or three adults in the congregation—a husband who had been conducting an affair, a businessman who was failing, a housewife who bemoaned the fact that she had refused a call to the mission field when she was young—but never, in all my memory, by one of the pillars of the church. They apparently considered it bad form to wear their Christianity on their sleeves or betray the possibility that they hadn't been living all out for God even without a revival.

I recall one frame in the movie of my memories of that church that suggests their unrelenting guardianship of the institution. It occurred following the most successful revival the church had had in years, one led by Dr. Wayne Dehoney, a charming evangelist who told winsome stories and had a way of connecting with every age group in the church. On the final night of the revival, he asked everyone who had made a decision for Christ during the entire two weeks of meetings to join others who were coming forward that evening. Then he asked for someone who cared about each person who had come—a parent or a friend—to come too and stand beside them as a sign of love and support. The line eventually stretched around the entire perimeter of the sanctuary. A "love offering" was taken that night for the evangelist and singer (as they called the visiting music director), and it was the largest ever received on such an occasion—more than $3,000, of which $1,800 would go to the preacher and $1,200 to the singer.

At the very next business meeting of the congregation, a week or so after the revival, one of the deacons rose to his feet and made a well-rehearsed little speech about the church's responsibility to the local economy and how it was important for the members of the congregation to support a motion to limit the amount of money that would be paid to preachers and singers in future revival meetings. The deacons had prayed about the matter, he said, and decided that the evangelist who was coming for the next revival should be paid a flat $1,000, which they considered ample, and the singer a flat $600. Both were still very respectable sums at the time, which was in the late 1940s. It wasn't right, said the earnest old institutional hawk, to lavish more on visiting leaders who had their own sources of income elsewhere while working a hardship on local merchants and the church's own budget. He didn't come right out and say it, but his implication was that people's tithes and offerings to the church would probably be lower because they had given so much to the visitors.

Ironically, the next revival was not nearly so successful. It was led by a more sober, meticulous preacher named Dr. Elwyn Wilkinson, who didn't have as many heart-warming stories and lacked Dr. Dehoney's talent for connecting with all kinds of listeners. And there was also the fact that the waters had been fished out, so to speak—that is, successful revivals rarely follow soon upon the heels of other successful revivals. This time when the love offering was taken it amounted to several hundred dollars less than the amounts promised the two leaders and the church had to make up the difference out of its own budget. So at the next month's business meeting another deacon rose to say that the deacons had prayed again, and this time they felt led to remove the stipulation of how much would be paid to future revival preachers and song leaders. After all, to specify how much the visiting leaders would be paid flew in the face of the very idea of a love offering.

Score another one—I think—for the institutionalists!

⌐⌐

Thinking about my old home church made me think also of an incident at the little Presbyterian church in our town. They had employed a very popular young minister named Rev. John Grimes. Grimes was more engaging and free-spirited than most Presbyterian ministers and was soon making the rounds of the civic clubs and schools, winning praise and commendation wherever he went. His sermons were fresh and his personality was effervescent. Soon some new people were making their way to the Presbyterian services, and a few of the elders in the church became concerned that their control over the congregation was beginning to erode. Thus they began to strategize about ways to curb the popularity of their new minister. A whispering campaign began to suggest that Rev. Grimes was perhaps a bit too cavalier as a pastor and tended to be neglectful of his more serious duties. One woman complained that on a very hot Sunday morning when she was fanning herself furiously with one of the funeral-parlor fans from the pew rack—there was no air-conditioning in those days—the pastor was walking up the aisle past her and she said, "Pastor, would you please open that window? I'm burning up."

"Would you believe it?" said the woman. "He said, 'Sorry, I'm not the custodian,' and walked on past me."

Stories of this kind circulated throughout the congregation, undermining the praise that Grimes was getting from those who genuinely liked him. One of the most universally damning reports had to do with his obsession with movies. He was always citing this or that line or story from a current movie in his sermons, as he had been advised by a seminary homiletics teacher that this was a good way to connect with one's audience. But in this case the practice backfired, because the elders and deacons of the church were constantly saying to one another, "I wish I had as much time to go to the movies as he does. We aren't paying him to spend his afternoons at the theater, are we?"

At last, when the elders thought they had enough grievances to force their young pastor's resignation, they called a special meeting of the session and presented him with a list of twenty-eight complaints about his ministry in their church. The clerk of session was Kenneth Gibbs, the owner-manager of the Somerset Undertaking Company, one of the most respected businesses in the community. Gibbs was a sturdily-built man of about forty-five, with dark hair and a handsome face. He was very quiet-spoken by training, but also very firm and forceful. It was he who conducted the meeting, offering a preamble and then handing the indictment list to Grimes. There were a few minutes of quiet during which time Grimes looked at the list, pondering it, and the eight or ten members of the session sat looking at him and then each other, trying not to smile or betray their sense of imminent success.

Finally Gibbs thought it was time to draw the matter to a close. "Well, what are you going to do about it?" he asked, expecting that Grimes had no other course but to offer his resignation.

Grimes looked calmly up from the list, laid it on the desk behind which he had been sitting, and with apparently naive dignity said, "Well, I guess there's only one thing I can do." The men looked at one another and actually broke into visible smiles. "I'll just have to ask you fellows to resign and I'll get me a board I can work with."

I love that story. I also love the ending of it. A few months later, Rev. Grimes did resign in order to accept a more lucrative position as chaplain at a mental hospital in Lexington, Kentucky. And the letter he wrote back to some folks in my home town, I heard, said that he was having a wonderful time at the mental hospital, because the people there weren't half as crazy as some of the people he had been forced to consort with in his parish!

☙

Control. That's what it's all about, isn't it? Who's going to run the institution? In an ideal church, the Spirit of God would be in control and would guide all the major decisions of the congregation. But in the average church—in *most* churches—the Spirit of God doesn't have anything to do with it. The dinosaurs do. The politicians and figures of power who think the church belongs to them, not to God.

A number of years ago, there was a novel by Gregory Wilson called *The Stained Glass Jungle* that was very outspoken about the way it is in the institutional church. In the story, Rev. Fred "Beloved" Worthington, an unctuous little butterball of a district superintendent, lectures Jack Lee, a young, idealistic minister, on the reality of life in the Methodist church:

> Possibly the first Christians *were* as selfless and unworldly as is generally assumed; certainly they were few in number, their organizational structure was quite modest, and they anticipated the end of history at an early date. But time went on, the church grew, its shadow lengthened, and the motives which had empowered a band of lay preachers in a temporary world soon proved insufficient for the full-time professionals of an on-going organization. So title and rank and salary and seniority had to be wedged in among love and sacrifice and faith.[1]

Elsewhere in the novel, Jack accuses Worthington of seeing no place for the Holy Spirit in cabinet meetings where ministerial appointments are worked out. "Of course it has a place!" says Worthington. "I've seen problems unraveled which could only have found solution through a wisdom more than human. I've seen the whole cabinet stop dead for prayer."

"But if a big church—" Jack starts to remonstrate.

"Oh, come, come, beloved!" says the D.S. "Everyone knows that the Holy Spirit has nothing to do with the big church appointments—those are all settled by wealthy laymen. But the Spirit certainly does exercise an influence in the medium and lower brackets."[2]

It was a knowledgeable Methodist minister who wrote the novel—his name wasn't really Gregory Wilson—and it is no wonder he preferred to publish it pseudonymously. He was certainly right when he said that wealthy laymen have a lot of control in the church. So do the politicians who have spent a lot of years cultivating their positions of leadership.

A United Methodist friend of mine named Jeff Baynes was assigned a few years ago to an attractive church in the town of Boaz, Alabama, a college community with a large, popular outlet mall. Jeff and his wife were happy with the assignment, as they had just come from a church where the financial restraints were so severe that Jeff was asked to do janitorial services for the church as well as be its pastor. I visited him in his new situation. It was a graceful church plant and we had tea in his office. He seemed quite content there, and said now nice it was to have several college professors in his congregation who could appreciate the finer points of his thoughtful sermons. In fact, he said he would like to stay there for the remainder of his ministry.

I was surprised, a few months later, to learn that he was being transferred to a church in Vernon, Alabama, a remote location next to the Mississippi border. What had happened? Some of the people on the Pastor-Parish Relations Committee had begun to complain about his ministry, he said. There wasn't anything very specific. They just didn't feel that he was "right" for the job, or that he would be able to help the church to grow over the next few years. Jeff did some research on the church's internal history. That particular parish, he discovered, had had thirty ministers in the last fifty years, averaging a turnover every nineteen or twenty months. As he talked with other ministers who had served the church and began to fill out the picture, what Jeff found was that the PPR Committee was very jealous of its power and prerogatives and wanted to keep them by frequently shifting ministers. If no minister was allowed to stay long enough to get a footing in the parish and community, they would maintain their hegemony in the congregation. The bishops and district superintendents were aware of what was happening, but had taken no action to curtail this disgraceful pattern. They didn't want to jeopardize the flow of money and support from a generous church.

⌇

District Superintendent Worthington, in *The Stained Glass Jungle*, says that the Holy Spirit operates best in small churches but that wealthy laymen control the larger churches. I had an interesting experience in my last parish, the Little Stone Church on Mackinac Island, Michigan, that clearly demonstrated the control of wealthy laypeople even in a small congregation.

Because the Little Stone Church is only a seasonal congregation, materializing in May and June and then dematerializing again in October to leave the island to the natives, who are almost all members of St.Anne's, the Roman Catholic church on the island, it has always remained relatively small. When I went there as minister, there were about fifty members. Most of them were far above average in wealth. Some had inherited money and property, while others were CEOs of large corporations who came to the island in the summers for its agreeable climate and pleasant ambiance. In general, I found them very casual about the church and felt that I had a free hand to craft the ministry as I thought best.

As the church building was designed and erected in 1905, when there was not even running water for an indoor toilet, there were no offices attached to the sanctuary. (A toilet and a large closet were later added to the rear of the building.) The minister was not expected to keep office hours, and there was no secretary. The only two members of the staff, in addition to the minister, were the organist and a wedding director. It was an ideal spot for a minister who liked to write and interact with members in a casual, ad-hoc fashion.

But I noticed, after I had been the minister for about five years, that some of the wealthy members of the congregation appeared to become increasingly uncomfortable with the changes befalling the church. My wife and I had become noticeably popular on the island, and we frequently had guests in the worship service from the Catholic and Episcopal churches. The membership roll had grown as a number of islanders flocked to the church. Some of these were wealthy and influential people, and others were not. Several were associated with the music department of the Grand Hotel, and others worked for various hotels and restaurants on the island. Additionally, there were hundreds of visitors to the island who came back to see us summer after summer, so that the capacity of the little building was often taxed by the crowds of people attending.

The church had always operated on the basis of a yearly call. That way they could easily control the pastoral situation. One year, when they had a very fine and influential minister who turned out to be an alcoholic and sometimes embarrassed church members by things he said about them, they simply took care of the problem by not inviting the minister back for the following year. In my case, inasmuch as I was not an alcoholic, they seemed happy to reissue the invitation year after year, and one year even begged us to return after we had decided not to.

But in my seventh and eighth seasons, I think a number of the old guard in the congregation were becoming extremely apprehensive of my popularity. They may also have been having second thoughts about my theology and politics as well, as the Island Bookstore was now displaying copies of my recent books, *God, the Devil, and Harry Potter* and *Ten Things I Learned Wrong from a Conservative Church*. In the seventh season, I took a public stance against the community's persecution of one of our members who had fallen afoul of a local tradition.

Mackinac Island is widely known for its refusal to allow motorized vehicles on its streets. Little is said about the hundreds of electric carts that transport paying guests around the golf courses or the hundreds of snowmobiles that the local populace employs to get around in the winter. But it has been a law on the island since early in the twentieth century that no cars, trucks, or SUVs are permitted on the island — only a police cruiser, an ambulance, and a couple of fire trucks are allowed. For some reason, one year the town council decided to enforce its ban on motorized vehicles by cracking down on four or five people who, for medical reasons, employed electrically assisted bicycles. To tell the truth, I had never noticed before this action that such bicycles even existed. Because they employ a small motor in one axle and a small generator in the other, they look almost like other bicycles.

It was a crazy thing for the town council to do. Within a few weeks of their issuing tickets to offending cyclists and confiscating their bikes, the ACLU and the Michigan Civil Rights Commission took up the cyclists' cause and a full-fledged PR war was soon being waged in the courts, the newspapers, and the evening news segments of the state's TV programs. Much of the publicity focused on a middle-aged man named Steve Christie, a musical entertainer at the French Outpost who with his wife owned Mackinac Island Florist, the most popular flower shop on the island. Christie's knees had been damaged in a car smash-up a few years earlier and he needed the electrical-assistance feature on his bike in order to pull the cart he used for delivering flowers. Photographs of him sporting a colorful shirt and standing astride his bike with the flower cart behind him appeared in dozens of newspapers, including the *Detroit Free Press* and the *London Times*. He became a poster child for the electric-bike riders and was execrated by the traditionalists on the island.

One Sunday while this legal battle raged, I preached a sermon called "Jesus and the Electric-Bike Controversy." My text for the sermon was Mark 3:1-6, the story of the Pharisees' anger when Jesus healed a man's withered hand on the Sabbath. I cited the hubbub over the electrically assisted bicycles as a way of getting into the sermon. Then I said it wasn't my business to say from the pulpit whether the use of the bicycles was right or wrong, as I had never tried to interfere in political matters from the pulpit. But the bicycle issue, I said, did illuminate the way people became worked up over the flouting of a tradition, because the keeping of the Sabbath was probably the most fiercely held tradition of the Pharisees in Jesus' day, and it might well help us to understand this particular biblical text more than we had ever understood it before.

I told the story of the man with the withered hand and of Jesus' sympathy with the man that led him to break the law by healing him.

I talked about the fanaticism of the Pharisees over the keeping of the Sabbath, and how they invariably stood with the law against any case of mere human need. Inevitably, as any preacher would, I painted the courage of Jesus in flouting the law as more worthy in God's eyes than the observance of the law. "That is a sad comment on the human condition, isn't it?" I said. "The tradition about the Sabbath—the law—meant more to these people than the miraculous healing of this poor man's withered hand."

I concluded the sermon by reminding the people that I was not bringing my own judgment to bear on the bicycle case: "As I said in the beginning, this sermon is not about our local controversy over whether people can use electrically assisted bicycles. It is about Jesus and his unvarying habit of caring more for people and their problems than he did about the law and traditions of Israel. If you want to apply that to the controversy about the bicycles, that is your business. But I have to warn you, after many years in the Christian ministry, that Christians don't always care what Jesus did when they make up their minds about how they are going to react to a situation in our day and time. It might seem logical that they would, but they don't. I just don't want you to be disappointed."

One extremely prominent local woman who was not a member of our church called up my wife immediately after she got home and said, "Your husband called us all Pharisees today!" She was a good friend of ours, but it was obvious that her toes had been stepped on. And looking back on the sermon, I realize that it stepped on an awful lot of toes that day and that some of the more powerful laity in the church probably began to whisper among themselves that it was time for me to go.

The bicycle controversy did not go away. When the ACLU and Michigan Civil Rights Commission won a legal decision in favor of the electric-bike users, the city appealed. It was spending money hand over fist. By the time the battle was over, the contest would have cost the city a third of a million dollars in lawyers' fees and court fees. There was a flurry of new publicity. The city lost the appeal. Then some intern at the newspaper discovered that the federal government had quietly passed a law some six months earlier that electric bikes up to a certain size were to be regarded as regular bikes. That ruling had come about because dozens of municipalities all over the country were suing to enforce a ban on electric bikes on public biking trails and were regularly losing their suits.

But the ire of Mackinac Island did not die away with the legal resolution of the battle. Posters appeared in the bank lobby and post office asking people not to patronize Steve Christie's business. Somebody paint-bombed his flower cart. His bike was disabled. Drivers for the local carriage business warned him to get off the island. He and his wife were so crippled financially by their loss of business that they sold their shop and moved to Tennessee.

During the summer of my sermon on the bike controversy, one couple in the church began attending a small Bible church that had started on the island a few summers before. Then another couple. It was easy to tell, from their remarks, that they were uneasy having a minister who was more liberal than they were.

☙

Two things happened at the beginning of the next summer, which was to be my last. One was that I related a cute joke about President Bush—a nonpolitical joke, actually, about the president's getting his come-uppance from a group of school children—to a member of the church's board of directors who had always been very friendly. He took immediate umbrage and fired back a long, vitriolic e-mail boasting of his patriotism and of having served in the armed forces. The second was that my wife threw a gala birthday party for me at the Grand Hotel on the island. All our church members were invited, and a number of old friends from former churches came, including several gays from our church in Los Angeles. None of the old guard church members even mentioned the party to us afterward, and that summer none of them invited us to dinners or other social functions.

In previous years, the congregation had always appeared to be in great anxiety about the possibility that we wouldn't return for another season. My wife and I were feeling so expansive from our party that we decided to agree early to return the following year. I even said, "We might make it two more years and round our tenure out to ten." I said I have always been into Hebrew numerology. So I wrote the chair of the pastoral committee soon after the party to say we would make it simple that year by saying before we were asked that we would be happy to return.

Silence.

The chairperson didn't write a note or call us to say she was happy with our decision. One day Anne ran into her as they were walking to a book group at a home in the woods. Nothing was mentioned about our returning.

At our next board meeting, I was a few minutes late, as it was held after a Sunday service and I had to stay behind a few minutes to greet the visitors. When I went in, I noticed that there was an awkward silence among the directors. Usually they were jovial and upbeat, but this time they were glum and subdued. I realized afterward that the moderator had already announced to them that I had notified the chair of the pastoral committee of my willingness to return. I can only imagine the conversation that ensued.

In the meeting itself, the moderator mentioned that I had written a letter to the pastoral committee saying I would come back, but didn't elaborate. Nobody said, "Great!" Nobody said anything.

I don't think I'm paranoid, because I'm enough of a mystic not to care about such things. But after a month had elapsed and nobody had mentioned our returning, I decided I had volunteered where I was no longer wanted. So at the next month's board meeting I apologized for getting ahead of the pack and withdrew my offer to return.

One board member who had been absent the month before protested. But the others were silent.

I knew I had been right. The so-called "powers that be" at the Little Stone Church didn't wish my services any more. They wanted to be in control again. I think they actually wanted the attendance to fall off so they could claim the services again as their own. They wanted to go back to the way it was in their little institution without the interference of an outspoken, liberal-leaning minister who befriended gays and people with electrically assisted bicycles.

I don't know what would have happened if I had not withdrawn my offer and they had been forced to expose their desire for me to leave. In a showdown, a majority of church members would undoubtedly have supported me. Half of them had become members under my pastorate. But it would have been a sticky wicket, and I'm glad I avoided it, for them as well as for myself.

The next minister the church hired was a nice man. We stopped by the parsonage the following summer to meet him and his wife and liked them both. People said he told a lot of jokes in the pulpit. He was also a former military chaplain. The institution would be safe in his hands.

Meanwhile, Anne and I have gone on with our lives, thankful that we don't have to pack up and make that long pilgrimage every spring with enough belongings to last us until we return in the fall. We understand what happened, even if people don't talk about it, and we're okay with it. We just wish the institutional figures could have been more open and direct about what they were doing. But maybe the fact that they weren't is a tribute to what the church had become for a brief interval in its existence—a real church, with integrity and spontaneity—and they weren't entirely happy to be giving that up.

The most damnable aspect of this whole institutional business is the way the average pastor is eventually co-opted by the institutionalism of the church he or she pastors. Some pastors resist it better than others, of course. I think of my old friend Don Shehorn, a Baptist minister from San Antonio who stopped by our home in Nashville years ago and then kept in touch with us for years. Don was a rangy, blue-jeaned man with unruly black hair and a loud voice that seemed to slip and skid a little when he talked, as if it wasn't always totally under his control. There was a bracing freshness about him. He had a kind of naiveté or openness that made him more interesting than other people, and when he talked it was with an obvious enthusiasm for life and its glorious rawness. Don's church was in Universal City, Texas, and had a lot of military personnel in it. He liked that, and liked Texas, with its sprawling, rough-and-tumble ways and the freedom he felt to express himself as a theological gadfly. I published one of his verse sermons in a volume I edited called *Experimental Preaching.* It was the early 1970s, and experimentalism was in the air.

But eventually Don began to feel hemmed in in Universal City, Texas, and moved up to Missouri. He pastored there a while, and one day he stopped to see me again and complained that church members expected too much of him, they expected him to say what they wanted to hear and not what he had to say as a prophet of God. So one day he walked out of the Missouri church as well and got a job selling cars. He said he could be more honest about the cars he sold than he could about the gospel the churches wanted him to preach.

Most pastors aren't that unconformable and they aren't that brave and independent. I remember that Disciples of Christ preaching conference in Missouri where I met the minister who had traded a 1500-member church for a 150-member church and was happy at the exchange. In earnest discussions at that conference, many ministers admitted that they didn't like all the hoops they had to jump through to keep their churches. I said, "Why don't you quit?" "I can't," said one frankly. "I have two children to put through college." "I wouldn't know what else to do," said another. "My wife and I need the insurance coverage," admitted another. There was almost an epidemic of honesty as, one after another, they confessed how much they would like to quit because they felt abused and prostituted by their churches, yet knew they were trapped because their jobs were more agreeable to them than anything else they were able to do. I felt very sad when I flew home from that conference.

How many ministers, I wondered, are dissatisfied with their congregations and yet feel chained to them the way abused spouses feel bound to their abusers?

I know in my own experience how subtly one can be suborned by the institution. It was my final Easter Sunday in the big church in Los Angeles. Every minister breathes a sigh of relief when Easter is over, for Lent and Holy Week are killers to ministers, just the way Christmas is. I was standing with other people in the lovely forecourt of our old church, feeling the warmth of a late-morning sun on my snowy-white robe. As we chatted, I noticed six men entering the forecourt from the direction of a city park. They looked like vagrants, with scruffy clothes, dark beards, and the shifty look that becomes a part of homeless people's mien when they get around normal folks. One of the men came up to me and asked if they could go into the sanctuary to pray. "It's Easter," he said. "We'd like to say a prayer."

I felt mixed emotions. I couldn't forbid them to enter the sanctuary, yet I worried that they were there for more nefarious reasons. Our church was in a changing neighborhood where it was always getting knocked off or vandalized. "Go ahead," I said, and then motioned to Manuel, our head custodian, who was standing attentively at the edge of the crowd. "Manuel," I said, "follow those men into the church and keep an eye on them, please." Manuel nodded. He knew what I was thinking, what I was worried about.

A few minutes passed and the men didn't reemerge. Neither did Manuel. I worried that the men might have slugged Manuel and proceeded to steal something, perhaps the morning offerings. I excused myself and slipped into the narthex. I looked through the small windows of the doors but couldn't see the men in the sanctuary. I pushed open a door and passed inside. Still nothing. Only as I walked down the aisle did I begin to discern that they were all in the chancel area of the church, between the pulpit and the pews, on their knees praying.

I was embarrassed by my own suspiciousness. The old church's institutionalism had rubbed off on me. I had become a protector of property.

Ashamed of myself, I moved among the men and asked their leader if they would like me to lead them in a prayer. He said they would. I laid a hand on his shoulder and another on the shoulder of one of his companions and offered a heartfelt prayer of thanksgiving for the life and ministry of Christ and for this glorious day of the church year when we celebrated his continued life in the world. I felt wonderful being among these poor men—far more wonderful than I had felt in any other part of the Lenten and Easter celebration. They were what the gospel is all about. Not mammoth old buildings and endless committee meetings and accountants' books and pro forma sacraments. Derelicts. People who had no real home, no money, no support in the legal, political, or religious systems of the day. These men who were shabby and dirty, and Christ who is risen and shiny. This was what it was all about, not the other.

I hope I never forget.

Two

To Most Churches, Appearances Are More Important than Reality

Surely everybody in the English-speaking world has seen at least one episode of the British TV comedy called "Keeping Up Appearances." Hyacinth Bucket (pronounced *booKAY*, as she is quick to say) is a middle-class housewife with delusions of personal grandeur who spends enormous amounts of energy trying to make the neighbors think she and her husband, Richard, poor sod, are elegant, highly regarded people who, but for the accidents of birth and place, would be at least minor royalty. She is always "mentioning" to people that her sister Violet has a Mercedes, a swimming pool, a sauna, and room for a pony, and is forever being thwarted in her efforts to keep her other sisters Rose and Daisy—and Daisy's Neanderthal husband, Onslow—away from her home and out of sight with their coughing and sputtering old clunker of a car. Hyacinth has become almost synonymous with vanity and pretense.

It is part of the institutional character of most churches that they too like to maintain certain appearances and care far more about what people think than they do about having a real passion for the Christian faith. They all want to have a good "show" on Sunday—an impressive service with a big choir; an attractive, rhetorically gifted preacher; and an air of Christian respectability—and look like a happy, prosperous religious community. They may in fact be roiling with feuds behind the scenes—in a processional at the National Cathedral in Washington, D.C., I once heard the archbishop caustically dress down a lesser cleric for being too far to the rear of the line, as if he were trying to impress somebody!—and essentially care nothing about following Christ or ministering to the poor of the world. But they have the institution's sure instinct for putting their best foot forward in public in order to make everybody think they are fulfilling their role as model churches.

Maybe this is one reason I have a lot of sympathy for Pentecostal churches. Since their beginnings at Azusa Street in Los Angeles early in the twentieth century, they have worn their storefront mentality as a badge of honor, glorying in God and not in the beauty of their sanctuaries and the elegance of their preachers. Pentecostal ministers don't mind standing on street corners to proclaim the kingdom of God or holding services in gymnasiums and warehouses. They realize that the Spirit of God can make a palace of any place, however humble, and that no church, however big-steepled, is really a church without the Spirit of God.

The reader may recall that one of my churches, the fourth, met in a schoolhouse. It would later own a nice building and begin to acquire the habits and pretensions that inevitably go along with such edifices, but during its tabernacle years when the appurtenances of Sunday school and worship had to be reassembled every Lord's Day, with baby beds, cribs, and hymn books being hauled in from cars and station wagons (the SUV hadn't been invented then), there was a delightful earthiness about the church, a sense of being close to God. We were still small then—fifty or sixty people in worship—and nobody knew for certain that our operation would fly. Suppose a few people became disenchanted and dropped out, or angry and stormed away, and we might not even be able to afford the nominal rent we were paying the school board for the use of their building. Churches have an appropriate humility at that stage. They don't take anything for granted, or assume they're God's gift to the community around them.

I admit that I missed some of the niceties of the established church—an office where I could hang my coat, counsel a church member, or use a private restroom before going into the service—and I would have liked to look up at stained-glass windows and not through the rain-streaked panes of plate-glass windows in aluminum casings. It would have been nice to have a regular kitchen with our own things in it, so we could store a big coffee pot and have an occasional luncheon or potluck supper. And on the Sundays when my sermon was weak or the song leader had a sore throat, it would have been helpful if we had been holding service in a regular sanctuary where the beauty of old wood, colored glass, and a mellow-sounding organ could have compensated for what we were obviously lacking.

But like the Jews in the wilderness, we would all look back on those days with a sense of nostalgia for the closeness we felt to God without the regular trappings of the church. A few years ago I was in Mobile to speak in a large downtown Baptist church and who should I run into there but DT Evans, the slight little man who had been our song leader at Raritan Valley Baptist Church in New Jersey. DT's wife Dot had died, his children had all grown up and married, and he had retired from his job with the government. With nothing else to do, he decided to take the position as head custodian at the church in Mobile, which was near where he and Dot had been living when she died. His face lit up as we reminisced about the church in the school house.

"This is a beautiful church," he said, gesturing toward the lovely sanctuary with its tall stained-glass windows, "and I love it here. But there was something very special about having church in a school. It was kinda bare-bones Christianity, and you knew everybody was there because they really wanted to worship and serve God. I've missed it ever since, and so did Dot!"

DT. wasn't a very good singer, and he wasn't a good song leader either. I don't know how he got the job. It happened before I came on the scene. I can still remember the way he scrunched up his face as he tried to reach the higher notes on the scale, and I would feel sorry for him that he was in so far over his head. We had a great vocalist in the congregation named Dean McAdoo, who had been a member of the Bison Glee Club at Oklahoma Baptist University and had sung all over the country. Dean should have been our song leader. I guess the thing about it was that DT. wouldn't have had the job in a normal church. There the congregation would have insisted on having a singer whose ability was commensurate with the beauty of the setting. But in a schoolroom it didn't appear to matter. There even DT could lead the singing. There has to be a lesson in that somewhere.

⇛

My next church, the big Presbyterian church in Lynchburg, Virginia, wouldn't have tolerated DT in that position. It was a real institution, and it mattered how things looked.

Herb Barks can attest to that. Herb had been the pastor there two or three ministers before me. Herb had had a wonderful education. His father was headmaster of Baylor School in Chattanooga, one of the finest prep schools in the nation, and Herb had gone there. I don't remember where he went to college and seminary, but I recall that he went to Europe for his doctoral work with one of the great German theologians. He had a church in Louisiana for a while, and then went to a Presbyterian congregation in Glendale, California, where he served with distinction for a few years. When the pastoral search committee at First Presbyterian, Lynchburg, did a national search for a minister, they discovered Herb and lured him to Virginia. Herb loved the beautiful sanctuary of First Church, Lynchburg, and anticipated having a great time as the minister there.

On his first Sunday morning, he walked down the wide center aisle behind the Chancel Choir, wearing his clerical robes, dark trousers, and brown shoes. *Brown* shoes. They would have been fine in California. Probably nobody had ever noticed what kind of footwear he wore in the pulpit there. But promptly after church his first Sunday in Lynchburg, two

fastidious little ladies, who were both Sunday school teachers and prominent women in the church, cornered Herb in the narthex and informed
him in no uncertain tones that the minister of *their* church *never* wore
brown shoes in the pulpit. Black shoes with black trousers and a black
robe. That was the order of the day every Sunday, without fail. Fifty-two
Sundays a year, except for vacation time, of course. Black shoes. It didn't
matter if they were wing tips or high-tops or loafers. But black shoes.
Never anything but black shoes.

Herb learned fast. He was no dummy. The next Sunday he had a shiny
new pair of black shoes on his feet. And he wore black shoes every
Sunday—until his last. His last Sunday at the First Presbyterian Church
of Lynchburg, Virginia, the Reverend Dr. Herbert Barks processed
solemnly down the aisle behind the choir, as his habit was, wearing a pair
of audaciously white sneakers!

I've always assumed that the white sneakers were Herb's way of
thumbing his nose at formal ecclesiology, at least for the time being. His
father had retired from the head-mastership of Baylor School, and Herb
had been tapped to succeed him. And from Baylor School he went on to
be headmaster of yet another private school in one of the Carolinas.
Maybe he had had enough of institutional Christianity.

It was more than the black shoes. Herb was a fun guy, but he was also
a serious Christian, and he expected churches to be serious about their
religion. Fortunately he had a sense of humor. It helped him to tolerate
the pretentiousness of the church he pastored.

He lived in Lynchburg during the tense days of racial integration. The
local newspaper, owned by the Carter Glass family, was extremely
conservative and was strongly opposed to the commingling of blacks and
whites. Jerry Falwell, whose Thomas Road Baptist Church lay on the
other side of town from First Presbyterian, was also outspoken in his
opposition to integration. God didn't want it, he was assuring everybody.
Later, when integration had become a fact of life, they both changed
their tunes and managed to forget that they'd ever sworn to fight it to the

death. But at the time the little city hard by the Blue Ridge mountains was a hotbed of reactionary talk and Herb Barks was one of the few outspoken advocates of integration as something Jesus would have mandated if he had been living in twentieth-century Virginia. Crosses were burned on his front yard—the bonfires of hatred—and on the church's lawn as well.

And Herb recalls the night the First Presbyterian session met, in the midst of all this tension, and the first matter to be brought up was sheep manure. Charlie Leys, who was an employee of the Leggett Department Stores, had come with an order from Mrs. Leggett, who was a member of the church, to get the session to pass a ruling that in the future only sheep manure would be used on the church's extensive rose gardens because she was of the firm opinion that cow manure was not good for them. Another man on the session (there were not yet any women on it)—Herb couldn't remember his name—was just as certain that cow manure was good for roses and sheep manure wasn't. So a prolonged argument ensued. It went on for nearly an hour before Bruce Thompson, who was manager of a three-state Coca-Cola bottling business and was an old country boy, became so impassioned about the subject that he forgot to use the word "manure."

Then it was "sheep shit" this and "cow shit" that, and, reinvigorated by this switch to earthier Anglo-Saxonism, the argument raged on for another forty-five minutes, when everybody appeared to have had his say, grown weary, and let the conflict rest for a moment. At that point, George Stewart, president of the First Colony Life Insurance Company and probably the wealthiest man in town, and also the only non-old-Lynchburger on the session (they could hardly deny such a successful man a prominent place in the church's government), opened his mouth for the first time to say, "Fellows, I'd like to say a good word for bull shit!"

Startled, the men began to laugh. Seeing the ludicrousness of the way they had spent most of the last two hours, they all cracked up and laughed and laughed. Then, drying the tears from their eyes, they had a benediction and went home.

I've always thought that was one of the best examples of institutional-ism I've ever heard about. Parts of several American cities were burning down over the integration question. Lynchburg was torn apart by it. And the session of the First Presbyterian Church spent nearly two hours debating about what kind of manure they ought to put on the church's rose garden! It was pathetic. And the saddest thing of all is that churches do this all the time.

My friend Walter Vernon loves to tell the story of a Congregational church in the vicinity of Hartford, Connecticut, where the younger people joining the congregation eventually outvoted the older people on the color of the sanctuary walls and changed them from white to some shade of pastel. Six deacons resigned in protest, and the controversy continued to swirl. Fearful that the entire church would disintegrate, the pastor called on Dean Harvey Potter of nearby Hartford Theological Seminary to come and speak on a Sunday morning. Everybody in New England Congre-gationalism adored Harvey Potter, and the minister thought he would surely help to quell the fury. The church was crowded on the Sunday when Dean Potter came, and everybody was eager to have his views on the new paint job. When the time for the sermon arrived, Dean Potter climbed the circular staircase into the high pulpit and for a moment simply stood there looking around the sanctuary. At last he spoke.

"Well," he said, "it was *worth* six deacons!"

He was joking, of course. But it was a joke designed to deflate an overblown conflict, one that had managed in the weeks of its raging to deflect the church from its primary *raison d'être*, to be a congregation of believers seeking to advance the kingdom of God.

These stories raise interesting questions. When is a church that looks like a church not being the church? And, conversely, when is a church that doesn't look like a church actually being the church? On paper, at least, the answers to both questions are obvious. In real life, it is harder to tell.

In the 1970s, I was fascinated by stories coming out of Judson Memorial Baptist Church in New York City. Howard Moody was the minister there then, and Al Carmines, who won an Obie award for his off-Broadway musical *In Circles*, was the minister of music. I was on a program once with Al Carmines and Madeleine L'Engle, the writer, for the National Council for the Arts and Religion. Al told us about what was happening at Judson Memorial. Pastor Moody had decided to take out all the pews so that the sanctuary could be used during weekdays for other, less obviously religious programs such as union meetings and gatherings of aspiring poets and playwrights. He said he thought the odor of stale sweat in the room made it a better theater for God on Sunday. Many uptight religious people were very opposed to what Moody did, of course. They saw it as a desanctification of what had always been holy and sacrosanct. But it was a matter of opinion.

The *Christian Century* ran an article by my college classmate Dr. Tracy Early purporting to be a visitor's guide to New York churches. There were many kinds of church experiences to be had in the Big Apple on a Sunday, said Early, and a range of preachers to hear. At Judson Memorial, he suggested, one might be treated to a sermon in the round or a colloquium on workers' rights, while uptown, at prestigious Fifth Avenue Presbyterian Church, one could count on hearing an elegant sermon from the tall, handsome minister, Dr. Bryant Kirkland, that would probably include "an edifying story from the life of President Eisenhower."

Bryant was a friend of mine too, and I preached for him two or three times and had coffee with him whenever I went to New York. Considering the more rarefied atmosphere of his upscale congregation, I thought he did a good yeoman's job with his preaching, attempting to bring comfort to the up-and-out without forgetting the number of young secretaries and office clerks in his audience every Sunday. As the old saying goes, "Different strokes for different folks." He and Howard Moody were probably both serving the Lord in their respective parishes and continuing to justify the thesis of Ernst Troeltsch's *The Social Origins of the Churches*, that we have different kinds of congregations because there are all kinds of people who need them.

Most churches lose a lot of opportunities to witness to the transcendent in our midst, but some appear to be almost terminally blind to it. Because they have become mere institutional shadows of the fervor that once brought them into being, they are satisfied with attractive buildings, well-adorned sanctuaries, busy programs, and going through the motions of Christianity without ever thinking reflectively and critically about whether they are truly following Christ. Whole generations of pastors and church boards go by without the kind of real challenging that keeps us on the mark as servants of the wordless Word. We become so attached to "things"—to our buildings and well-kept church rolls and five-year plans and reputations in the community—that we seldom think about whether it is all worth it in the eyes of God.

According to the Gospel of John, Jesus, after he had been raised from the dead and joined his disciples by the Sea of Galilee, asked the penitent Simon Peter, "Simon, do you love me more than these?" The demonstrative pronoun "these" is often assumed to refer to the other disciples—did Peter love him more than James and John and the other fishermen? But in the Greek it is actually a word that indicates something nonhuman: "Do you love me more than these things?" Possibly Jesus was gesturing at the boats and nets that were the staple of a fisherman's life. Did Simon Peter care more about his Lord and the gospel than he did about the life that had drawn him back to Galilee after the crucifixion?

The same might be asked of any church. What do we love the most—our soaring towers, our expansive programs, our esthetically designed services of worship, or the Christ who started the whole thing all those years ago and his radical ideas about including the poor and outcast in the kingdom of God? It is a penetrating question, and one we are usually loath to ask.

The book of Revelation didn't hesitate to ask it. In fact, it was the essential question that lurked behind the accusations against various churches: Ephesus, that it had abandoned the love it had at first; Pergamum, that it harbored heretical teachers; Thyatira, that it had a Jezebel in it who spread lust and fornication; Sardis, that it had a name for being alive but was really dead; and Laodicea, that it was neither hot nor cold in its religion, but only lukewarm (chapters 2-3). Clearly the Christians in those churches did not love Christ more than other "things."

One modern writer who raised the question brilliantly was Charles M. Sheldon, the Congregationalist minister in Kansas who on a series of Sunday evenings read to his church the chapters of a book that would become world-famous as *In His Steps*. It was in the years of the Great Depression, and Sheldon was concerned that the church was merely doing its business as usual without showing enough passion and concern for the millions of poor and starving people of America. So he wrote a novel in which a tramp steps up to the chancel at the close of a Sunday morning worship service and asks the minister for permission to address the congregation. The tramp is actually a printer by trade. For several months he has been hiking across America, looking for work so he can send some money home to his family. He looks out at the congregation and accuses them of not really caring for the poor around them. He has been in their town several days and few people have even spoken to him. They have no idea, he says, of what it means to be homeless or to have so little money that you can't afford pictures on your wall or a piano on which to give your children piano lessons. If Christians were really serious about following Christ, he adds, they could eliminate poverty and hurt and mistrust in the entire world. Having said this, the man collapses and is carried to the parsonage next door. A few days later, he dies.

The minister of the church, the Rev. Mr. Henry Maxwell, is so moved by the tramp's extraordinary words that he invites interested members to join him in reflecting on the man's words to them. He challenges those who come to pledge with him that for the period of one year they will not take a single important action or spend a single day without first asking themselves, "What would Jesus do?" Soon there are hundreds of people in the community who have taken this pledge. The entire town is transformed by their actions. A newspaper editor changes his paper's policy toward the kind of articles it will print. A businessman alters his company's practices on labor and transportation. A popular local singer decides not to accept an offer to go on the stage. A medical doctor begins spending more time with charity cases. Even the minister, Henry Maxwell, draws up a new manifesto about his pastoral work, and recommits himself to being a figure of love and healing in the community. The stranger's "sermon" to them has found lodging in their hearts, and they commit themselves to making the reality of their faith more important than the appearance of it.

It is to the credit of many people that they were challenged by Sheldon's book —it has been a religious best-seller for years—and the idea of asking "What would Jesus do?" (WWJD) has in fact become a familiar set of initials on pins and banners in recent decades. But it is sad to think that the reason the book and the reminder of WWJD are so provocative is that most churches are exactly like the one with which Sheldon began his story—groups of people meeting socially under the name of Jesus but without much consciousness of what it means to do that.

☙

While I was writing this chapter, I had a phone call from my longtime friend Dr. Thomas Greene, a Baptist minister in North Carolina. Tom wanted to know what I was doing and I told him the theme of the chapter. He laughed and recalled a woman in one of his churches who said to him at a farewell party as he was leaving that parish, "Dr. Greene, I've always appreciated that your shoes were well shined." There was nothing, he said, about how he had visited the sick and cared for grieving families and tried to preach good sermons. It was only the glow on his shoes—his appearance—that she noticed.

I thought about Herb Barks's brown shoes and the tennis shoes he wore in rebellion.

To many people, these are the things that are important about a church. Not whether the church is ministering to the poor and hungry, not whether it is looking after its elderly, not whether it is helping its children to blossom spiritually, not whether it is teaching people to pray and share and love one another, not whether it is using its funds responsibly for the kingdom of God, but whether the minister looks presentable and the worship is entertaining and the building reflects their status in the community.

Tom Greene fully understands this. He has Parkinson's disease, and it has progressed so far in recent years, even though he is only fifty years old, that it sometimes causes him to tremble and interferes with his speech. When it first became apparent to others, in his church in Raleigh, North Carolina, the church members were very sympathetic. One Sunday when he began to shake so badly as he preached that he had difficulty speaking, two deacons strode down the aisle in his direction. "Oh my," he thought to himself, "they are going to take me out of the pulpit and I will never come back again." But the men entered the chancel and stood, one on either side of him, bracing him so that he could not shake any more, and held him rigidly until he had control of his body again and could complete his sermon.

"Don't worry, pastor," they assured him, "we're here whenever you need us. We'll all get through this together."

Tom was deeply moved by this expression of love and loyalty, and I was greatly impressed when he told me about it. "This is the way Christianity ought to be," I said to myself.

But the love and loyalty were too good to last. Eventually a little group of dissidents began to insist on Tom's resigning so the church could hire a new minister. They had nothing against him, they said, but they didn't believe the church could survive in the competitive world of churches with a pastor who was handicapped by such a devastating physical disability. Some of Tom's friends assured him that he shouldn't worry, it would blow over. But it didn't blow over. The dissidence spread through the congregation. Finally Tom had to negotiate a date for his resignation and the promise from the church that they would continue to pay him for six months beyond that date if he failed to find other employment. He didn't find other employment. The church had only reflected the harsh realities of the business world and its treatment of the disabled.

I told Tom during the process of his adjustment that I could see the side of those who argued for his leaving. The minister is *the* speaker for a congregation, the one who more than any other person voices the thoughts, beliefs, and ideas of the church. If he or she is unable to do this with at least a modicum of ease and ability, there is a sense in which the church itself is paralyzed and cannot move forward. For a crazy moment, I recalled some experiments being conducted by biologists at George Peabody College for Teachers back when I was a professor across the street at Vanderbilt University. The scientists were severing the facial muscles of rhesus monkeys that had clearly been the dominant monkeys in their tribes. Once these muscles were cut, the monkeys could no longer lead and were soon deposed. It would be wonderful if the church could be more tolerant of its ministers' problems or shortcomings—I wish it could—but it is understandable when it can't.

I couldn't help wondering what Jesus would command in such a case and how differently the church might behave if he were visibly here and in charge of it.

⌇

Tom's case reminds me of a minister I met once when I was speaking for the Northern Illinois Conference of United Methodist ministers. Someone had told me that this particular minister's wife had experienced a severely disabling stroke a few months ago, so I sought him out at lunch to give him an opportunity to talk to a sympathetic stranger. I asked how he was doing. "OK," he said, "but it has been pretty tough." "What's the hardest part?" I asked. He continued to eat for a moment without responding. Then he said, "The worst part has been my church's reaction." "Oh?" I said.

His wife had her stroke the day before Christmas. It left her paralyzed on one side and unable to think or speak clearly. Therapy had helped a little, but not much. She could no longer function on her own. At first, he said, the members of his congregation were very empathetic. They brought dozens of casseroles, sent flowers, offered to help in any way they could, and set up a relay team for bringing food and driving his wife to the hospital. Most importantly, they assured him that he should take all the time he needed to be with her and see that she was well cared for. Their church was not large and did not require a lot of oversight. So he often spent a couple of extra hours at home in the morning and returned an hour or two earlier than usual in the afternoon in order to care for her. Everybody seemed kind and understanding.

For a while.

Then the whispers began. The pastor was spending too much time with his wife. He was neglecting the work of the church. He was not visiting the sick and shut-ins as often as they thought he ought to. He often seemed tired and ill prepared on Sunday morning. The parish work was piling up. The church was falling behind on its budget.

It wasn't long before the district superintendent confessed that a little delegation from the pastor-parish relations committee had been to see him about getting them a new pastor. When the D.S. didn't deliver as fast as they expected him to, they went to see the bishop. Their church was languishing, they complained. They had been tolerant of the pastor's situation, but they couldn't go on much longer the way they were going. Something had to be done. The bishop had to step in and reassign their pastor to another post.

It hadn't happened yet when I was talking to the minister, but the bishop had spoken to him about a staff position at another church. It would be easier for him, in a way, because he wouldn't have primary responsibility for the operation of the church. But he was dreading it. It meant making a move, and he worried about how his wife would get along in the new situation. She would be leaving behind most of the people who had known her when she was well. Who would really care about her in the new community? For that matter, who would care about him? It would be the first time since they married that he had to take the major responsibility of preparing for the move. He admitted that he was depressed and didn't know how they were going to make it.

I understood the church's position. The ministry is a very demanding role, and when the minister is unable to fulfill it, it is natural for people to become concerned and nervous and want to make a change. But it is so thoughtless, in a way—so sub-Christian in an organization that is devoted to loving and caring and telling the world about the importance of love and care. If a minister can't find the help and support he or she needs in the church, where can it be found?

Again, the church wants to appear to embody its own preaching. But does it? Sadly, I'm afraid, it doesn't. In fact, it very rarely does.

༦

The most dramatic example that I know of the church's failure to live up to its own teachings—or at least of a highly placed church member's failure to do so—occurred in my Los Angeles parish on a Thanksgiving Day. We had just completed our annual Thanksgiving worship service, which we billed as "The Mayor's Thanksgiving Service" because Mayor Tom Bradley, the great African-American athlete-turned-politician, came every year and sat on the front row as a sign of his blessing for all the different groups who gathered to celebrate together. Our church was part of the Mid-Wilshire Association of Churches and Synagogues, but this service was always held in our sanctuary because (a) it was the largest one available and (2) Congregationalists have always believed they *own* Thanksgiving. It was always a high point, because the flags of the various churches were carried down the aisle with the Torah scroll from Wilshire

Temple, where the great Harvey Fields was then the rabbi, and the preaching duty rotated year-by-year among the various ministers, priests, and rabbis.

The service that day had been especially limpid—strong and clear and joyous, with everybody participating warmly and exuberantly—and some of us were standing around outside in the beautiful autumn sunshine, chatting until nearly everyone had left. Suddenly on the edge of my perception I saw an unkempt figure materialize from the direction of a nearby park. He was gaunt and haggard, with an aureole of thin, unwashed hair circling his distressed-looking face. He had not shaved for several days, and the stubble of beard on his face was encrusted with blood. Even though it was a warm day, he clutched a heavy mackinaw around him, as if he were freezing. It was soiled, and, like his face, stained with blood. He had no shoes. Instead, his feet were wrapped in plastic bags that were held in place by rubber bands. "I have AIDS," he announced without preamble. "My folks kicked me out. I got mugged in the park last night. They took my wallet and my shoes. Do you have anything to eat?"

We didn't. There had not even been any cookies on the coffee table that morning. But I went inside and got him a cup of coffee, and poured lots of sugar and cream in it so that he would have some extra calories.

While I was gone, he admired a beautiful cloisonné pendant my wife was wearing, and asked if he might touch it. She held it out for him to feel. Emboldened by her kindness, he said he had not been hugged in a long time, and he desperately needed to hug. Would she please hug him? Fighting back the tears, she opened her arms and cradled him as if he were one of her own sons. Would it be all right if he kissed her, he asked. "Of course," she said, and held him again as he planted a tender kiss on her cheek.

While I was getting the coffee, I phoned a hospice that wasn't far away, one where we had sent two or three other people in need of a home when they were sick or dying. They said they had a bed for him, and were about to serve the Thanksgiving meal if he could be there soon. So I called for a cab. It arrived just after he finished drinking the coffee. I put him in it, gave the driver the address of the hospice, and paid him in advance. I told the man I would come by to visit him in a day or two.

We drove home then, our bright, clear day not as bright as it was before. Somehow it was going to be hard to have a happy Thanksgiving after that experience. When we went into the parsonage, the phone was ringing. Anne picked it up, hoping it was one of our children. It wasn't. It was one of the vice presidents of the church's Women's Association.

"I just want you to know," she began, "how badly you have just disgraced your husband and our church!"

Anne was baffled. What was she talking about?

"You know very well what I'm talking about," she fairly shouted. "I saw— we saw—that man you were hugging in front of the church. He was only a street person. It was obvious he wasn't one of us. What were you thinking? How could you behave that way in front of our church?!"

"But— but—" I heard Anne's attempt at protestations. She tried to explain that the man had AIDS and was dying, that he had been robbed and beaten the night before, that his parents had turned him away, that he was alone and friendless in the world, but obviously the woman wasn't listening or wasn't hearing. The tirade went on and on. Anne was shaken when it was over.

She didn't understand. The church was supposed to *look* as if it was concerned about Jesus' little ones, not actually do anything about them. The minister's wife was only to *appear* interested in the poor, not actually put her arms around them. Even if we feel pity for the world around us, and want very badly to do something for it, we must remember that we represent an important institution and not be carried overboard by our emotions. It is the *appearance* of charity that counts, not the real thing.

God forgive us.

╰⌒

I know it is natural for people to want to appear better than they are. And, as churches are only collections of people, they too want to look better than in fact they are. The urge is documented beautifully in an article in The *Atlantic* by Walter Kirn called "Lost in the Meritocracy: How I Traded an Education for a Ticket to the Ruling Class." Kirn, a professional writer, tells how he finessed his way from being a smart kid in Minnesota to getting into Princeton, then going on to win a prestigious Keasbey Foundation scholarship to Oxford. As he progressed, he became more and more adept at shilling people, conning them into thinking he was bright and knowledgeable, while, inside, he became less and less a real person. The full weight of the contrast hit him the summer before he left for Oxford, when he went back home to Minnesota for a visit and found himself sitting one night with a high school friend in a pickup truck parked next to the river.

The friend's name was Karl, and, while most of Karl's classmates had left home to go to school, he had elected to stick around and help his folks with their dairy farm. But he had also been reading—omnivorously, apparently—and thinking about life. When he heard that Kirn was back in town, he had looked him up, eager to have a conversation with somebody who had been off at school and learned a lot of things. Since everybody had left town, Karl said he hadn't had anybody to talk to about art and literature. He was eager to have a deep discussion.

"So what are your views on Emerson?" he asked. He figured that he and Kirn had a lot in common.

"But we didn't, in fact," writes Kirn, "and I didn't know how to tell him this. To begin with, I couldn't quote the Transcendentalists as accurately and effortlessly as he could. I couldn't quote anyone. I'd honed more-marketable skills: for flattering those in authority without appearing to, for ranking artistic reputations according to the latest academic fashions, for matching my intonations and vocabulary to the background of my listener, for placing certain words in smirking quotation marks and rolling my eyes when someone spoke too earnestly about some 'classic' work of 'literature,' for veering left when the conventional wisdom went right and then doubling back if the consensus changed."3

Kirn had learned a lot of things since he'd left Minnesota—irony, flexibility, class consciousness, the ability to get along with his peers and those above them. But he had not really loved art and life and literature the way his old friend Karl had. He had acquired the skills of deception and pretension, of taking a few shreds of knowledge and information and parlaying them into a career based on those skills. He didn't admit this to Karl. That was one of the things he had learned—not to confess his real faults, the gigantic ones that lay like enormous fissures at the bottom of his facile public persona and glib way of talking about culture.

Later that summer, something happened that was decisive in Kirn's life. A month before he was scheduled to fly to England to take up his life at Oxford, he came down with a cold that turned into pneumonia and forced him to stay in bed for a couple of weeks. One night he was restless and found himself standing in front of the bookcase where there was a row of handsome volumes his mother had bought when he was small. He had never bothered with them then, regarding them as primarily decorative, but now he picked up *The Adventures of Huckleberry Finn* and did "something unprecedented" for him: he carried it back to his bedroom and actually read it all the way through, from cover to cover, every chapter and every page. A few days later he repeated the act with *Great Expectations*, another classic that he had made it through Princeton without ever opening. The experience didn't change him immediately, he says, but it started a process that eventually saved him from his snobbish, pretentious beginnings and turned him into a person of genuine learning and curiosity.

Most people in churches, like most people everywhere, are a lot like Kirn. They learn a way of sailing through life with certain phrases, attitudes, and unexamined perspectives. Most of them become fairly adept at a kind of Christian posturing, appearing shocked at certain words and behavior, affecting a life of prayer and devotion, nodding their heads at certain things the preacher says, shrinking in horror from the idea of an evil world where drugs, crime, and pornography prevail, and chattering innocently and naively about life and its meaning, always prefacing their remarks with "The Bible says." And for most of them, most of the time, this is sufficient. They don't really want to know more or go deeper. Like the church people at the start of *In His Steps,* they are content with what they know and how they behave. The thought of a more radical discipleship never enters their heads, or, if it does, they manage to dismiss it abruptly, fearful of where it might lead.

I said I have always had a soft spot in my heart for Pentecostals and others who don't set as much stock by appearances as most Christians do. I really admire my friend Jim McReynolds, who for years has pastored little congregations of folks who haven't made it very well in the competitive world. Jim, who has a doctor's degree in ministry from Vanderbilt Divinity School, has bipolar disorder. For years he managed to curb it or hide it when it couldn't be curbed, and looked as if he was going to set the world on fire as a preacher and a writer. But eventually the tension beat him down and he had to settle for different goals. He is more like a race horse than a plow horse—he can cover short sprints with incredible speed and beauty but he can't go the distance. He has pastored several churches and held a number of counseling positions. But in his latter years he has spent a lot of time with congregations of rejects—spastics, burn-outs, retards, people with Alzheimer's. He is like St. Francis of Assisi, only with wounded people instead of animals. They don't affect their Christianity. There isn't anything pretentious about their worship services. People drool, interrupt the preacher, rattle in their plastic sacks for a bottle of water or a bag of chips, get up and amble around the room.

For some reason, I think the presence of Jesus is stronger in their midst than it is in the finer churches of Christendom. At least what you see is what you get. There is absolutely no tension between appearance and reality.

Three

Every Successful Minister Is Drowning in a Sea of Minutiae

Years ago, in the headier, more affluent days of book publishers, I received a complimentary monthly magazine from Foyle's bookstore in London called *Foylibra*. Actually, it had another name, but Foyle's always put its own cover over the original and that was the name by which I knew it. I liked the magazine especially for the witty comments of one particular reviewer, who was almost always caustic but also right on target. His name was Auberon Waugh, and I think he was a cousin of Evelyn Waugh, the famous novelist.

I remember one review of his in particular, which made me howl with laughter when I read it. It was a double review, in which he dispatched two books at once. One was by a prominent Anglican bishop and the other was by Marjorie Proops, a Miss Lonelyhearts columnist for one of the London tabloids — the *Mirror*, I think — and each consisted of letters the writer had received and the answers that had been posted back to the authors of the letters. Waugh tore the bishop's book to shreds — no, confetti! — ridiculing it for its vacuity and pomposity, and highly praised Miss Proops' book for its freshness, cleverness, and sensitivity to the letter-writers' feelings and predicaments. He concluded his review by saying that he was not going to throw away the bishop's book, however execrable he had found it, but would keep it lying on his bedside table in case he were ever tempted, in the middle of the night, to reconvert from his adopted Catholicism to the Anglicanism he had grown up in. The bishop's book, he was certain, would remind him of why he wanted nothing else to do with the church of his childhood!

I refer to this image with the thought that I might do as much, now that I am retired from the ministry, by keeping the diaries of my pastorates on my nightstand so that I should never be tempted to return to the work I was doing. I have had occasion recently to review them and was overwhelmed by the sheer, unadulterated busyness they chronicled. How in the world, I wonder now, did I ever manage to have a sane thought about anything, much less compose a meaningful sermon and prayers for the Sunday services? No matter how clear my calendar at the beginning of a day, or how uncluttered my desk, I never got through the hours without looking like a man who had wandered, lost and desperate and starved for water, through a field of sticktights and cockleburrs! I cannot believe, in retrospect, how I lived through the experience.

Take this sample day from one of my Los Angeles journals:

6:00 a.m. – *Morning prayers*

6:30 a.m. – *Showered, left for breakfast at Dupar's with PR committee; discussion of whole PR picture; Diane C. wants me to write weekly column for L.A. Herald-Examiner*

8:30 a.m. – *Met with Virginia S.* [my secretary] *and cleared calendar for interviews*

10:00 a.m. – *Staff planning session, with Nancy W.* [principal of Pilgrim School] *present*

11:30 a.m. – *Met with Walt V., Tom S., and Peter N.* [other ministers on staff] *to discuss plans for Advent*

12:30 p.m. – *Lunch at CNA with Tony & Elizabeth C; discussion of next month's Women's Association meeting*

1:45 p.m. – Dictated letters until 2:45; interrupted twice by people
who "just needed a minute"

3:00 p.m. – Drove to Cedars of Sinai to visit with Gladyce and Paul
W.; Paul not doing well

4:00 p.m. – Drove home, worked until 5:30 on message for bulletin

5:30 p.m. – Swam until 6:00, then showered and dressed for dinner

7:00 p.m. – Anne and I met Pat and Jim H. for dinner; talked
about Cedar Lake and the church camp

10:30 p.m. – Home; answered three phone calls; chatted a few
minutes before going to bed at 11:15

c–ɔ

I usually stayed home on Monday morning and wrote my sermon for the next Sunday. And I tried to take off one day a week, usually Friday or Saturday, depending on a number of variables, to do something relaxing and pleasurable with my long-suffering wife. But this kind of schedule was not at all unusual for the other days of the week. In fact, many days were even more hectic. Most of them became a blur: one thing blended into the next all day long, so that it wasn't always easy to remember them all to record them in my diary.

It hadn't been any different at Lynchburg, my parish before Los Angeles, except that there I spent less time on the streets getting from one place to another. I remember one day in that parish when my secretary buzzed me to say that a man had driven a hundred miles or more to meet me and asked if I could see him despite the fact that he didn't have an appointment. I had just finished my counseling sessions for the morning and didn't happen to have a lunch appointment, so I told her to send the man in and go on to lunch if she liked. He was an Episcopalian businessman from northern Virginia who wanted to talk about going into the ministry. Somebody had given him a book of mine. He had liked it and thought it would be good to consult with me about his desire. I asked what he presently did. He ran a company that outfitted the interiors of ocean liners. I asked how he could do that where he lived, as it was more than a hundred miles inland. He said that they manufactured all the pieces and then transported them to the shipyards for installation.

"Why do you think you want to become a minister?" I asked him.

"I sometimes go down to our little Episcopal church and sit and meditate," he said. "I enjoy the peace and quiet of the church—the way it is here now. And I love to read. If I were a minister, I'd get a lot of things read."

I laughed out loud. I couldn't help it. He had come at lunch time, when all the secretaries and other ministers downstairs had gone out and things were relatively quiet in the building. I picked up my calendar from the desk and joined the man on the sofa to show it to him. I don't remember precisely what was on it for that day, but it probably included meeting with three or four staff members about different things—in larger churches, staff members probably consume more of the senior minister's time than parishioners do—and having at least one committee meeting. I had probably already been to the hospital once—fortunately, in Lynchburg, it was just around the corner from our church and I usually walked—and would drop in again that afternoon to see which new members had been admitted. On a typical day I would have had to submit copy for the Sunday bulletin or the church newsletter and possibly give an interview to one of the local reporters who liked to keep up with the ongoing war between the pastor and the fundamentalists. I usually spent two or three hours a day meeting with individuals who had requested a conference, and often had drop-ins in addition to those. And, though that day was an exception, I often had lunch with two or three people, either to check up on parishioners or do planning work with committee chairs.

"You're lucky today," I said. "I didn't have a luncheon date or I couldn't have seen you. Why don't we go grab a bite of lunch and we can talk while we're eating?"

All the way through lunch, the man kept saying, "But I don't understand. I thought ministers had a lot of alone time and could tend to their souls."

I said that maybe they did in small Episcopalian parishes but that he should check with the minister of his own church and see if his impression was correct even there. "Most ministers are pretty busy," I said. "They're like the housewife whose work is never done."

When we got back to the church, I gave him another book I had written, *Christ and the Seasons of Ministry*, shook his hand, and told him to get in touch with me any time. I never heard from him again. My guess is that when he got over his shock he opted either to stay where he was or to enter a monastery.

It's true. Most ministers are among the busiest people I know. They don't always appear to be busy, because they learn early on to try to live casually each day. They have a lot of interruptions—I once preached a sermon on "Those Blessed Interruptions!"—but they try to remain flexible and make time for anybody who needs them. They have a lot of bosses—a number roughly equivalent to the church membership—and they try to be polite and listen to all of them. They have to perform an incredible variety of tasks, from visiting shut-ins to writing prayers to chairing meetings to calling on potential church members to marrying folks. And somehow, along with all of these things, they have to find time to keep abreast of developments in theology and biblical studies, write challenging sermons, attend more lunches and dinners than most people ever dream of, attend their children's ball games, and remain a tiny bit human.

It's a tall order, and most ministers live with the feeling that they're a day late and fifty dollars short on everything. Every minister I know says that he or she needs the first week of vacation just to unwind and stop feeling as if his or her life is going to be interrupted by somebody needing something. I often took my vacations in England or France so people wouldn't call me back to conduct a wedding or a funeral, and, as my wife will testify, I usually wrote five or six sermons while I was gone. Otherwise I wouldn't dare to come back, because my desk would be so piled up with things to do that I wouldn't have time to think about sermons for the first few weeks.

I thought I was busy when I was a professor in the divinity school, because, in addition to teaching a full load of courses, I wrote a book or two every year and was off to speak at some church or university once or twice a week. But the change of pace was so breathtaking when I went to my Lynchburg parish that I soon began to feel numb in my own spirit, and worried that I was losing my ability to feel and enjoy life. A psychologist I consulted as a *quid pro quo*—she had come to me several times for theological understanding—suggested that I begin making a note of any-thing during the day in which I felt a twinge of joy. It was a wonderful suggestion, and soon I was managing at the end of the day to recall as many as ten or fifteen truly joyous moments—things like seeing the dawning sun in the window glass, hearing a bird singing in the bush out-side our kitchen, watching a child throwing snowballs, and feeling warm and happy as I talked with one of our older members. But it really scared me at first, when I feared that becoming a pastor again had really screwed up my life as a human being!

∿

I mentioned that other staff members can be part of a minister's burden. It's true. Ministers who don't have a secretary or a co-pastor or other staff workers often think that if only they had these partners in ministry everything would be easier and better for them. But they're simply unin-formed. Don't get me wrong. I truly enjoyed having colleagues in min-istry. I was fortunate, in both of my larger parishes, to have prodigiously efficient secretaries who were also wonderful human beings. I don't know how I would have managed without them. And I had some delightful ministerial assistants and ministers of music to work with. They amplified my life enormously, and I look back on our associations and feel extremely gratified to have known them and had the privilege of working beside them.

But in my other churches except for L.A.—all five of them—I didn't have even a part-time secretary or an office in the church, and I found it terrifically liberating. At the personal level of writing sermons and prayers I got an awful lot more done. I used to have a friend named Bob Landry who was one of my doctoral students while he pastored a rather large Disciples of Christ parish in Knoxville, Tennessee, and later went to be a minister in Austin, Texas. Bob was extremely gifted and articulate, and had a first-rate analytical mind, and he was always talking about writing a book. His thesis on Harry Emerson Fosdick, which I supervised, was a fine piece of research. "If I only had a full-time secretary," he often declared, "I would write my book and be on my way!"

I suppose Bob thought a secretary would relieve him of the tedium of typing a manuscript and perhaps even help him with his research. I don't know. But I always told him, "Bob, I write a lot of books, and I don't have a secretary." We had two young secretaries at the divinity school to do the work of sixteen professors, and they were so inexperienced and inadequate that I never used them. One professor of New Testament who did, Leander Keck, later the dean of Yale Divinity School, got back a letter he had dictated to someone and found that the secretary who typed it had spelled "pentateuch" as "penny-took." It was a good guess, I suppose, but he rewrote the letter himself before sending it.

Staff personnel in the church are just like staff personnel in other institutions— they become jealous of fellow workers, they feel that they are being treated unjustly, they complain about working conditions, they are always looking for raises, they get involved in various kinds of misconduct, and they are often simultaneously obsequious to and resentful of their bosses. So the senior minister in most churches often winds up being a de facto CEO, the one at whose desk the buck stops, who must iron out problems before they turn into monsters or result in mutiny.

In one of my churches, I had a young associate minister who postured a lot and was always whining about how inferior other staff personnel were, then came running to me if he felt insulted or belittled by anyone in the congregation. One Sunday he burst into my office a few minutes before the eleven o'clock service livid with rage. He had been speaking to a senior men's class during the Sunday school hour and one of the men, a retired school teacher with a military bearing, had publicly dressed him down for his posture at the podium and his failure to project his voice so that everyone could hear. He reminded me of a six-year-old who comes in from school fuming about what some child said to him on the way home.

We had, in the same church, a young woman as minister of education who was adored by the young people and was a superb educator. But she also had a foul mouth that she didn't always successfully control. One time she turned to a doctor who was on the Christian education committee overseeing the youth work and told him frankly, after he had made some remark, "That shit won't flush!" The doctor was good-natured, even though he was shocked, but other adults in the church weren't always so tolerant, and I spent a lot of time preventing her being fired.

In another church, I had an associate minister on staff who was a triple-threat problem. First, he brilliantly ingratiated himself with several old-guard members of the congregation, feigning a devotion he lacked and buttering them up about their denominational loyalty during a period when the denomination was going through several real trials. Then he undermined me with those same members, suggesting that I did not have a background in their denomination and did not appreciate what they had been through. And finally he was like a rooster in a henhouse, cooing and stroking every female who didn't have a man or wasn't happy with the one she had. This was ironic, because he was physically one of the most unattractive men I ever met. Yet he managed to keep several romantic pots boiling most of the time, and I was forever having to deal with petty jealousies and broken hearts.

If I had had the power to fire the man, I would have done it on several occasions. But one of the damnable things about church politics is that in many churches the chain of command is set up to prevent the senior minister from having the power to hire and fire staff. The reasoning is that a senior minister can be jealous of a younger staff member who preaches better than he or she does or who cultivates a larger following in the congregation. In such cases, the senior minister ends up being an ethics cop and a shoulder to cry on without the authority to do anything about the problems presented by erring staff members. I confess that I heard with some satisfaction after I left that church that this particular associate had been caught embezzling large sums of money from the church treasury. But because he had made such close alliances with several powerful members, he was allowed to repay the money and remain on staff. He eventually left that church. I don't know where he is now, but I'm confident that, wherever it is, he is continuing his deceitful, under-handed behavior just as before.

There is a saying among ministers that the music department is the war department of the church, and there is a lot of truth in that. Because there are always a lot of people involved in the musical programs of larger churches, representing a lot of families and coteries of friends, the possi-bility of making a major blunder and having it spread like wildfire in the congregation is always present.

I made one huge misstep in my Lynchburg parish. We had a fine organist and choirmaster who served as minister of music. He grew up in England, where he played the organ for movie houses in the days of silent films. Thus he was a master of improvisation and capable of a wide range of musical presentations. Moreover, he was witty and quite likeable, and I enjoyed being with him. But he was in his middle seventies (his application, which I retrieved from the files, would have made him only seventy) and was slow-ing down a lot. He had become very impatient with youth choirs and had a way of discouraging participation, so that each year we would begin a new youth choir program only to have to close it for lack of support.

The older musicians in the church were becoming anxious about this, as they realized that the young people weren't receiving the kind of training that would make them good members of the adult choirs. So the church's music committee, which was comprised primarily of people associated with the choir programs, decided that we needed a new minister of music and came to me to handle the problem. I knew that this man was older than he had admitted, and figured that they were right, it was time for him to think about retiring. So I invited him to lunch one day and was trying to think of a way to handle the situation without hurting his feelings. He handled it for me by blurting out, after we had given the waitress our order, "You want to talk about my retirement, don't you?"

I assured him that everybody loved him, it wasn't that, it was the neglect of the young people that worried the committee, and said he should defuse the complaints by setting a retirement date at some time in the future. "It will take six months to a year to find an adequate replacement," I said. "Why don't you set your date a year from now and then everything can be readied for the transition?" He agreed, we enjoyed our lunch, and that was that.

Not quite. He had married a much younger woman, a member of his Chancel Choir who then advanced to first soprano soloist, and she was not prepared to have a retired husband. When she heard the news, she hit the ceiling. Within twenty-four hours, she had stirred up such an uproar that people from the music committee—the very ones who had asked me to bell the cat for them!—were complaining that I had acted arbitrarily and behaving as if they had had nothing to do with the matter.

I lived hard after that until that minister of music was gone and another was installed. Every Sunday morning, I got glaring looks from the minister of music's wife and other women in the choir as they processed by me into the chancel loft. It would have been easy to back down and say I had made a mistake. But I had agreed with the committee that it was time for a change, and I was stubborn enough to hold out until we had it.

⤳

Next to the amount of energy required for a minister to deal with staff members, that required for ministering to the elderly and the ill is probably the greatest. I've always been an old-folks junky, so that was never an onerous part of my duties in the ministry. It took a lot of time to call on the elderly—I tried to get around to all of them at least once a month—but it was always fun and encouraging to me. We had a lot of older women in our church in Lynchburg, and one woman in our L.A. church, Elma Corning, lived to be 113 and was for a short time the oldest woman in the United States. These women were almost invariably happy and delightful to be around. Maybe it was because they no longer had any great responsibilities. But they loved to talk, and especially to pick the minister for any gossip he might know.

We were fortunate in my Lynchburg parish to have a beautiful retirement home called Westminster-Canterbury only half a mile from our church. Westminster-Canterbury is the name of a cooperative venture in which the Presbyterian and Episcopalian churches establish joint highrise care facilities for the elderly, and there are several of them in the country, all thoughtfully arranged and well managed. I stopped at WC almost every day to see someone, and at the same time was able to visit with half a dozen others as I strolled through the lounges or dining halls. Periodically I led the weekly worship service at the home, which gave me an even greater chance to interact with all our members who were there, as well as with friends of theirs who were eager to meet their minister.

My wife and I still laugh about one such occasion when I preached at the home's monthly communion service. The ushers handed trays of bread down the rows of seated participants, and then trays of cups. In the middle of this solemn time, we heard a plaintive voice in the middle of one row exclaim, "I didn't get any!" Apparently the woman had been asleep when the tray went past her. An attentive elder who was serving at the end of the row passed the tray again, whispering to the woman beside her to hold it until she had finished and let her replace the cup before sending it back. When the woman had drunk the grape juice from the cup, she tried to force it back, not in the open place where it had been but on top of a full glass. The resultant pressure sent juice flying like a miniature gusher in all directions, anointing the women beside her and the man in front of her as well as the woman herself!

As I have said, the hospital where most of our members went in Lynchburg was only a short walk from the church, and I went there almost every day and sometimes twice a day. We normally had six or eight members in the hospital at any given time, except during flu season, when there might be a dozen or more. I usually spent less than five minutes with a patient, as we made it a policy not to take up their time from other visitors or to interfere with the medical or nursing staff, but still, considering the fact that I often had to wait a few minutes before entering a room, it took me an hour or more to make the rounds. One young associate once marveled that I could do it so quickly, so I offered to go to the hospital with him and give him some pointers. I learned that he was copying down all the room numbers, then following them seriatum until he had completed the list. It was a simple thing to show him a more efficient way. I led him to the farthest patient on the top floor, did that floor completely, took a flight of stairs down to the next floor, and so on. He was amazed at the difference it made, and was as pleased as if I had shown him a better way of playing mumblety-peg.

In Los Angeles, our members lived over a widespread area with a radius of at least fifty miles. We had one couple who commuted regularly from Las Vegas, Nevada. Because of the inordinate amount of time required to travel from hospital to hospital—very few members ever went to a hospital within a twenty-minute drive of the church—we had a minister of visitation who did most of the sick calls except for those involving the most prominent members of the congregation or close friends of the senior minister. I probably spent almost as much time doing hospital visitation in L.A. as I had in Lynchburg, but saw only three or four persons a week.

Both in Lynchburg and in L.A., I always felt refreshed by visiting people in the hospital because it was invariably an opportunity to minister at a time when people really needed it. I had some real moments of epiphany while standing outside hospital doors waiting to be admitted. There was nothing to do at those times except pray and meditate, whereas working in the office at church afforded very little of that.

The saddest times, of course, were when people were actually dying or had just died, and it was necessary to spend some time with their families talking about the loved ones and attempting to comfort and console them.

☙

Any minister can expect to devote a significant amount of time each week to funerals and weddings. Weddings are almost always planned in advance, and ministers can block off parts of their calendars for counseling, planning, rehearsal, and wedding, as well as for any meals or celebrations they will be expected to attend. But funerals usually come unexpectedly, and therefore often seem to happen at times when the ministers' schedules are the most chockful of other things. Still, they are among the most important work the minister does, and can never be hurried, neglected, or shortchanged because of that.

I have known some ministers who were very jealous of their weddings and funerals, and never liked for associates to handle them. I, on the contrary, was always happy if another minister on the staff had been closer to a couple and they wished him or her to marry them, or if one had known a parishioner so well that he or she was an obvious choice to take the lead in the person's funeral. But more often than not people wanted the senior minister to do the honors at either of these occasions and it was almost impossible to delegate them.

Once, early in my Lynchburg ministry, it became necessary for the church to juggle its calendar in behalf of a visiting speaker who had been engaged to come for several days, and this in turn necessitated my shifting my vacation time, which I had planned to take in England. A wedding had been planned for the period when I would have to be away, but I thought that would occasion little difficulty inasmuch as I had never known the bride and groom and one of the associate ministers in our church had been a close friend of the bride before she moved to another city. So I telephoned the bride and proposed that her friend take their wedding. She was delighted and said she really preferred that but had been afraid to ask. Her parents, who were still members of the church in Lynchburg, however, had other feelings. They felt that it would be "undignified" for anyone less than the senior minister to conduct their daughter's wedding service, and our relationship was definitely soured by this turn of events for the remainder of my years as their pastor.

Funerals can take hours out of the minister's work week, requiring several visitations in the home, talking with loved ones about choices of hymns and scripture readings, preparing remarks that are relevant to the deceased's life and character, showing up for the wake, conducting both a church service and a graveside service, and then being available to the close family members as much as possible for several days after the funeral. Sometimes funerals can be problematic, too, especially if there are any family feuds or disagreements involved.

Once I conducted a funeral for a woman whose twin sister wanted her buried in the family vault in Nashville, Tennessee. Her husband insisted that she be buried with his family in Salem, Virginia. Although the three of them—the deceased, her husband, and her sister—had been the best of friends during her life, her death had precipitated a major quarrel, and the husband and sister were not on speaking terms. I could feel their frostiness toward one another through the funeral itself, and by the time we reached the burial plot in Salem, Virginia, almost two hours away from Lynchburg, I had concocted an idea.

The woman had been cremated and we were about to inter her ashes. I drew the director of the funeral home aside and asked if there were any law preventing the separation of ashes about to be committed to the earth. He said there was none of which he knew. So then I got the husband aside and asked if he would have any objection to his wife's sister having some of the ashes to bury in Tennessee. It was clear that he was happy to consider a way out of their impasse and said that he would be agreeable. I asked the sister if she would like to have part of her sister's ashes to take to Nashville. Her face brightened as if the sun had just come out on a cloudy day.

The cooperative funeral director brought out another urn from one of his funeral cars and he and I supervised the division of the remains. We had a lovely service interring one of the urns, while the sister stood happily grasping the other one. Afterward, the husband and the sister embraced and walked off toward their respective cars in a mood of joyful reconciliation. I felt very Solomonic as I rode home.

As inconvenient as some funerals can be, however, it is the weddings that often become the *bête noire* of a minister's existence. One minister I knew in Birmingham, Alabama, told me that he spent an average of thirty-six hours a week on weddings, including the counseling that accompanied them, the rehearsals and rehearsal dinners, and the weddings and the celebrations that followed them. "I'm cursed to have one of the loveliest churches in the city," he said. "If our sanctuary weren't so pretty, maybe more of our people would go somewhere else to get married!"

He had a point, as I was to learn when I became a minister in my final parish, at the Little Stone Church on Mackinac Island, Michigan. Mackinac is a natural wedding destination for a lot of people anyway, largely because it doesn't allow motorized vehicles on its streets and the white wedding carriages pulled by beautifully groomed horses are like something out of a dream. And the Little Stone Church, sitting on the edge of a golf course with the governor's mansion on a hill behind it, is easily the most picturesque place on the whole island for a wedding. When I first went to the church, we were conducting three and sometimes four weddings a week. The church had a rule that every wedding must be attended by a man or woman from the congregation who would act as a facilitator, and when the women, who did most of this work, became tired of having to do it so often, they asked for a ruling that would limit the number to two weddings a week except in unusual circumstances, plus any vow renewals the minister was willing to take on. Believe me when I say that I appreciate what the minister had to say about all the time he spent on weddings!

Weddings are normally beautiful occasions, worthy of tears of joy. But as any minister will tell you, they can also be a pain in the neck. Often they involve split families that aren't getting along. I vividly recall one wedding in which the mother of the bride, wife number one, was incensed when the father of the bride arrived at the church with wife number two, who was considerably younger and flashier than number one, and sat near the front of the church. Wife number one stood to her feet and in tones that could be heard a block away demanded that he remove "that woman" from the church before their daughter arrived in her coach to be married. Sometimes weddings involve a bride and groom who aren't getting along. That's really sticky. I remember one wedding rehearsal, at night, when the groom-to-be didn't show up. One of the groomsmen went to fetch him and returned, saying, "He's with his mother and doesn't want to get married." The bride collapsed in tears. At this, her father, who was seated near the back of the sanctuary, began to vent his anger on the daughter, saying she didn't have any sense and shouldn't have chosen the young man she chose anyway. I went back to try to calm him, and he ended by stomping out of the church and saying he was leaving for the mainland and the others could come with him or not as they chose. His wife was rather nonchalant about the whole thing.

"He'll have a hard time doing that," she said. "The ferries have shut down for the night."

Rehearsal dinners were always one of the banes of my existence as a minister. I attended some that were quite lovely and touching, with endearing things being exchanged between the bride and groom and their families. But others were horrible, especially when they involved a lot of drinking and the bride and groom's young friends arrived from distant colleges and proceeded to make toasts or merely to offer observations in a loud voice that were quite embarrassing to everybody present. One groomsman once gave a little recitation of all the young men the bride had slept with before discovering that she liked the groom better than the others. I wanted to sink through the floor for the bride's parents. I even wanted to do it for myself!

Aside from all these time-consuming activities, every minister has to spend at least a few hours a week talking with church members who have some kind of burden they need to share, whether it is real or psychological in nature. Those who came with real problems never bothered me. I was always glad to be there for them and to put an arm around them and say, "You're going to get through this, with God's help." It was the ones with psychological problems who were the biggest drain, because they often came repeatedly and could never really get on top of their situation, whether it involved anxiety, jealousy, paranoia, or some other form of mental ailment. Women going through menopause often came and cried about their husbands' lack of affection and men who were having business troubles came and cried about their bad fortune. One woman who had managed to keep her son with her until he was almost forty came regularly to complain about how the son's wife was treating her. It was almost always some barely perceptible slight, but to her it was an insult to end all insults. A beautiful Japanese woman whose husband had died several years before I became her pastor came frequently to extol her dead lover and tell me all his better qualities.

One of the strangest cases I ever had occurred in Los Angeles. A woman came to me to complain that the young woman who lived with her was acting very strangely and ask that I talk with her. I said I would be happy to do that, and asked her to check with the young woman to see when would be a good time. "Oh, I mean today," she said. "Right now!" "Can she come now?" I asked. "She's at my house," the woman said. "I'd like you to go home with me."

I knew the woman rather well and realized she wasn't inflating the problem, so I told her I would go as soon as I had taken care of two or three things I had to see to before leaving.

When we reached the woman's home, she slipped a key in the lock and led me into the living room. We heard the young woman coming from another part of the house. She was singing. And when she got in the living room, she was totally naked. It was obvious that she was having some kind of experience. I had asked her friend if she was taking drugs and she said no, she thought that was the problem. She had a medical condition and sometimes failed to take her prescribed medicine. I tried to talk to the young woman and see if I could take her to the doctor, but she was manic and would have none of that. At one point she went into the kitchen and returned with a huge knife.

I went to the phone and called the police. They wanted to know if the woman had any relatives who could commit her for analysis. I said they all lived out of state. It took me several minutes to convince them to send a squad car to help. I also called my wife. I asked her to phone back every few minutes to be sure we were all right. After two or three calls, the young woman filled a bathtub with water, carried the phone into the bathroom, and dropped it in the water, together with a boxful of Oreo cookies.

When the police finally arrived, she was sitting at the grand piano, playing and singing at the top of her voice. One of the policemen said, "Why, she doesn't have any clothes on!" What a Watson he was! At last we managed to get a blanket around her and bundle her into the backseat of the police car for a trip to the hospital. By then it was past supper time and I gratefully turned the car in the direction of home.

I had barely got into the house when the phone rang. The woman who had asked me to see her friend was on the line. "She's back!" she howled desperately.

"Back?" I said. "Why?" The police had received a more urgent call as they were on the way to the hospital, and as the young woman was behaving placidly they took her home and dumped her out and then sped on to answer the other need.

So I had to return to the home and spend another two hours getting a police captain and his men around to the house. This time we were ultimately more successful. She was sedated and spent a couple of nights in the hospital, her medication was adjusted, and she was able to go home and function all right.

Later, knowing that I had helped her when she was literally out of her mind, she asked if we could have lunch together. We did, and she asked me, somewhat hesitantly, "Did I say anything I shouldn't have when I was out of my head?" I smiled and said, "No, I can't remember a thing you said."

Satisfied, she ate her lunch happily and we never spoke of it again.

❦

The point of all these things is that, whether they are funny or sad, boring or exciting, the minister is a very, very busy person. Nothing that is said in seminary is ever enough to prepare future clerics for all the things they're going to encounter. I went to one of the best divinity schools in the country and I learned a lot of things. But I was never shown how to conduct a wedding or a funeral, wasn't ever warned about the extreme demands on my time, and didn't hear word one about how to order my schedule so I'd have time to write sermons, prepare formal prayers, answer beaucoup letters, and conduct a budget drive while doing everything else. I suppose it was simply assumed that we would learn when we had to and that until then we were better off not knowing. Or else, as I've suggested, the professors themselves had never had the experience and didn't have the first whiff of an idea about how to pastor a church.

Maybe if lay people knew what churches do to their pastors, how they put them in an office and zap them to death with piddling little tasks that make it finally impossible for them to discharge their larger callings with anything like panache or distinction, they would take over the management of the church in a real hands-on way instead of merely trying to run it from the boardrooms. There have been a few large, important churches where this has been tried. Riverside Church in New York City is one of them. John D. Rockefeller, who built that noble edifice beside the Hudson, understood about business and decreed that his pastor, Harry Emerson Fosdick, should be freed of all the small stuff so he could concentrate on being one of the great preachers and spiritual leaders of America. It worked. Fosdick's sermons from the 1930s and 1940s are still among the most listenable and moving homilies in modern history, and Riverside Church became one of the foremost gathering places for Christians in the country.

Then, in the 1970s, Ernest Campbell became the preaching minister of Riverside. He was a Presbyterian minister with previous pastorates in York, Pennsylvania, and Madison, Wisconsin, and was accustomed to being head of staff as well as the preaching minister. ("Head of staff" is an actual Presbyterian term for the pastor.) Campbell chafed at not having control of everything—the pastoral work, the church plant, the whole enchilada. He argued, fought, and cajoled until the trustees relented and made him the operations director as well as the preacher and leader of worship. Within six months of getting control of everything, he was on the verge of a nervous breakdown.

I was in charge of the Cole Lectures at Vanderbilt Divinity School one year, and talked Jarrell McCracken at Word, Inc., the Christian book and record publisher, to sponsor the lectures and turn them into a major conference for ministers from all across America. I invited Ernest Campbell to come as one of our preachers, along with University of Chicago historian Martin E. Marty and several other important figures. One day I went by Campbell's motel room to pick him up. He was pacing the room like a worried tiger and jabbering about how impossible his job was. On the last day of the conference, Campbell and Marty were to join several of us for lunch at a steak house called The Peddler. The anteroom to the restaurant was dark and we had to wait ten minutes for a table. Campbell said he couldn't wait, he couldn't stand to be in such a small space for so long. I tried to calm him but couldn't. He was practically climbing the walls, and insisted on being taken to the airport. The man who was to convey him after lunch said he would take him on then, without any lunch. Within a few months, Campbell had resigned from his pastorate, the first minister in the history of Riverside Church to leave before he was of retirement age.

I have always believed it was because he had not been up to the demands of the job once he had succeeded in getting everything centered in his office. He had a good thing going when he went to Riverside. He should have left it the way it was. Ministers are human beings and can bear only so much pressure. Preaching a great sermon week after week is a drain in itself. Add to that the composition of prayers, the conduct of weddings and funerals, leading a staff of fellow ministers and secretaries, participation in boards and committees, a full load of counseling and visitation, numerous duties in the community, a sizable correspondence, and the toleration of fools and enemies, and you have a prescription for disaster.

Yet that is what almost every senior minister I know has to do. It is exciting to contemplate. Every young minister dreams of heading a big church and a commensurately sized staff. But in the end it is a spirit crusher and few ministers survive in such a pressure cooker for very long without losing the edge and vitality from their preaching and ministry in general. Most become spiritual hacks, CEOs who manage to look as if they're fulfilling the obligations of their callings while deep inside they're voicing the confession of the little cleric in Georges Bernanos's *The Diary of a Country Priest*, "I am no longer fit to guide a parish. I have neither prudence, nor judgment, nor common sense, nor real humility. God has punished me. Send me back to the seminary, I am a danger to souls."[4]

Four

Pastoral Search Committees Seldom Know or Tell the Truth

I learned the hard way that a minister should never put much trust in what he or she is told about a church by its committee to find a new minister. I hate to think that such committees actually lie—they're almost always composed of respectable, attractive, and likeable people—but something almost always happens to them when they serve with a group charged with finding their church's next minister. For starters, they begin to believe all the PR stuff about their church—its history of high-mindedness, commitment to missions, reputation for honesty and openness, and eagerness to embrace people of all races, creeds, and backgrounds. Then, as their search progresses and they tell their story over and over, they begin to idolize their church and imagine all that it *could* be with the right leadership. And finally, when they begin to close in on the candidate they're all agreed is *the one*, they become a lot looser with the truth, like a bunch of car salesmen salivating over a gullible customer.

Small churches rarely get into such a sales fever. They tend to say to a possible future minister, "Well, this is who we are. What you see is what you get. But we like you and would like to offer you a job." With larger churches and longer searches that almost always involve casting a wide net and then having to sort the fish that are drawn into it, however, there is invariably a tendency to romanticize the situation on offer. And the longer the search drags on, the more extravagantly romantic and glorified the situation becomes. If every church member in their congregation was as brainwashed and expectant as these search-committee members appear to be, it would be the kind of church to which no minister could ever say no!

༄

I can't count the number of times I've been lied to by a search committee. Not just from the churches whose positions I've accepted, but from a lot of churches I turned down. I remember a Baptist church in Houston, for example, where the committee bragged and bragged about how "open" they were, and how much freer they were than other Baptist churches in the country. Then, on our way to the airport, a bit of the truth inadvertently slipped out. I was sitting in the front seat by the driver, and my wife was in the back with two women from the committee. They began reminiscing about their experiences on the search committee, and talking about other candidates they had interviewed. One of them mentioned a particular candidate in a slightly pejorative tone. "Oh," joined in the other, "we could never have taken him. He said he wasn't sure if he believed in the Virgin Birth!"

My wife said she mentally checked off that church the moment she heard that. As for me, I was thinking about a friend who had been forced out of a Baptist pastorate in Waco, Texas, because he thought his church was pretty liberal—it was, after all, a large, university church—and he confessed one Sunday that he didn't think it was necessary for people to believe in the Virgin Birth in order to be saved. The guy who told the Houston committee he didn't believe in it was lucky that he said it when he did. He might have been called to that church and admitted it later. Then he would have had to look for another church—and would probably have kept his feelings about the Virgin Birth private the next time around!

Then there was the committee from a church in Richmond, Virginia, that told me what a great missionary church they were. I was glad to hear it, I said. But I noticed that they kept talking about how expensive their church building was, and the fact that it was constructed of handmade Williamsburg bricks. Why was it important, I wondered, that they were handmade? There was also a lot of talk about what an egalitarian church it was, in spite of the fact that it was in one of the most exclusive neighborhoods in Richmond and the building had cost so much money.

But we saw the truth about that when we were having lunch with the committee at the Williamsburg Inn—they had arranged to hear me preach in the Williamsburg Baptist Church—and one of the ladies noticed that there wasn't a butter knife beside the table knife in my wife's place setting. She lit into the black waiter as if he had committed a lynching offense, and a couple of the other women clicked their tongues in agreement. Anne picked up her table knife and began applying butter to her roll with exaggerated enthusiasm. "Oh, we never use butter knives at home," she said, smiling broadly at the waiter. "No point in washing an extra piece of silverware!"

Egalitarian, my foot!

Later, when I examined a copy of the church's annual budget, I noticed that they gave less money to missionary causes than they spent on caring for the azaleas and rhododendrons in their lovely gardens. They may have thought they were a benevolent congregation, but it was a benevolence like that of so many self-congratulatory donors—a mere pittance compared to what they lavished on their own comfort and entertainment.

Another time, I interviewed with a large church in Michigan that was looking for a minister. The chairman of the search committee was the president of a university in the same city as the church, and all of the committee members were impressive in individual ways. One of the flags that went down on the play for me was the fact that the minister who was retiring had been at the church for thirty-five years. Lyle Schaller once wrote that any minister who follows a minister who has been at a church for more than fifteen years and has either died or retired is only an *interim* minister, whatever he thinks he is. There is a great deal of truth in that statement. Long-term ministers have accrued a lot of loyalties in their congregations, and church members have a hard time dealing with their grief when those ministers leave. Comparisons, while they are supposed to be odious, are nevertheless inevitable. And even if the supplanting ministers are better, smarter, and more compassionate than the ministers they replaced, people will have a hard time agreeing that that it is true. They will *talk* about the new minister, and will constantly analyze him or her, almost invariably with negative results.

"Oh, Dr. So-and-so is eager to retire," the committee members assured me. "He has been here a long time and has a lot of friends in the community, but he realizes that he is getting too old to minister the way he once did and he wants to stop now so he and his wife can enjoy the years they have left. He will be very supportive of any new minister we get."

Ha!

I made it a point to meet with Dr. So-and-so while we were visiting the church. My wife and I met him and his wife for lunch one day and had a two-hour conversation. They now lived on a farm thirty-five miles from the church, and he came into the city only twice a week—once to preach on Sunday and once to play poker with some of his friends. He was proud of the fact that he could run the church from that poker game—that he discussed important church matters with his buddies and they agreed to take care of whatever he wanted handled in his absence. At one point in our discussion, Dr. So-and-so banged the table with his fist and said, "This is *my* church and it will *always* be my church!"

So much for the committee's promise that Dr. So-and-so was going gracefully and wouldn't interfere with the work of the new pastor. In my final exchange with the full committee, I turned them down and told them that the new minister, whoever they got, was going to have trouble with the former minister. They laughed and said they knew Dr. So-and-so, and he had assured them he would go along with whoever they chose. I heard later that the minister they selected stayed in his new post only six months, and Dr. So-and-so crowed very triumphantly when he left.

I interviewed for the senior minister's position at a large church in Minneapolis where the retiring minister had been at the church for twenty-five years. He was a very distinguished man, both locally and in larger circles. Yale Divinity School had once offered him a position on its faculty, but he had turned it down to stay at the church. It was a very fine church and I was strongly attracted to it. Its minister of music was a person of great renown and its choirs—particularly the large senior choir—were often judged to be the best in their region of the country. The congregation was large and represented a wide range of professions and backgrounds. Its worship services were grand and moving. The sanctuary was one of the most beautiful I had ever seen, with an exceptional warmth for its great size. In addition to the usual ministries, the church also had an art lending library to encourage people to enjoy the works of the great painters in their homes and a comfortable 281-seat theater that staged four original plays a year. The senior minister was extraordinarily well compensated. In addition to his salary, he was sent on an annual trip around the world to review the church's missionary work in schools and hospitals in Europe and the Orient. The chairman of the search committee was a professional headhunter and really did his homework. I was flattered to be at the top of the committee's list.

But again I was leery of following a strong minister who had been in the church so long. I met with him and he struck me as a man who genuinely wanted to cooperate with the new minister and make his or her task easier. He had read some of my books and announced, both to me and to the committee, that he was eager for me to be his successor. He was already planning to take a year's trip around the world when he retired, so that he would be out of his successor's hair during the most crucial time of realignment. And the committee was very reassuring. "Dr. C. has had a long and respected ministry," they said, "but he is tired and wants to lay his burden down. He likes you and will be extremely supportive."

Maybe, I thought. In the end, I did not feel led to take the church. I turned the committee down twice, in fact. I wasn't exactly sure why.

Mostly, it was because I didn't feel God's leadership to accept it. But probably my unconscious mind was warning me about the kind of problems I might have with Dr. C.

In this case, the new minister who did come to the church stayed two years. Two very *embattled* years. At the end of one year, both he and the congregation were anxious for his departure, but he had nowhere to go. So he managed to negotiate for a second year while he searched for a new position. The date of his impending departure was announced, but he had some grace time to arrange a move. I remember that on hearing the news I felt vindicated in my decision, and grateful that I had decided as I did.

But a few years later, I felt even more vindicated.

I was the Bible lecturer for a national meeting of the denomination to which the Minneapolis church belonged. I talked about a new interpretation of the Gospel of Mark, and how it hung on the realization that the story of Christ's calming the sea in Mark 5:1-22 is in fact a post-resurrection story. Dr. C., now retired for more than a decade, was present and took exception to the fact that I did not regard the resurrection of Jesus as a fairy tale. He not only took exception, he became quite livid about the matter. I attempted to have a balanced conversation with him, but it was impossible. We were diametrically opposed on one of the major theological and philosophical tenets of the New Testament. I breathed a belated sigh of relief that I had not attempted to succeed him in the church in Minneapolis. Obviously, given his long tenure there, he would have had many followers in his opinions about the resurrection. My life as his successor would have been hell.

Search committees may think they know their own churches well, and in some ways they undoubtedly do. But there are also certain vital points that they almost never know with any accuracy. They have witnessed everything in the congregation from a safe distance, as lay members, and do not understand that the chemistry can be quite different for the incoming minister. A new minister is in many ways like a new spouse in a large family—he or she is going to be observed with a passion-infused thoroughness that will not only be unnerving for a while but may actually result in explosive differences.

☙

The search committee of the First Presbyterian Church of Lynchburg, Virginia, where I ultimately had a very successful pastorate, was one of the smoothest and most attractive I ever met. They had spent two years in a national search and had actually called someone who agreed to come, but, faced with leaving a congregation where he had many strong ties, he had what was effectually a nervous breakdown and was unable to fulfill the agreement. My name was given to the committee at this point by Mrs. Mary Cosby, a nationally known inspirational speaker whose husband, Gordon, was the founding minister of the Church of the Savior in Washington, D.C. Mary and I met when we were both on a program for the Georgia Conference of United Methodists. Her brother-in-law, Jack Cosby, was chairman of the search committee in Lynchburg. Jack and his wife, Anne, came to Gatlinburg, Tennessee, where I was speaking to the Tennessee Association of Christian Churches, and persuaded me to visit Lynchburg to see their church and visit with the committee.

My wife, Anne, said to me when we first went to a meal with the Cosbys in Gatlinburg that I shouldn't be encouraging them, as we had almost decided at that point to permit the search committee from the First Congregational Church of Los Angeles to put my name forward in that venue. But Jack had such a winsome way about him—I have described him elsewhere as a kind of Sam Waterston figure with features more rugged than Waterston's and a manner more convincing—that I wasn't able to resist his entreaties. "It won't hurt to take a look at their situation," I argued.

The committee couldn't have been more welcoming or eager to please if it had been straight out of Mayberry on the *Andy Griffith Show*. The members, who ranged in age from a woman in her eighties to a young man sixteen years old and included a nuclear engineer, a doctor's wife, a teacher, a retired teacher, a secretary, a financial adviser, a manufacturer, a student (the sixteen-year-old), and Jack himself, who was president of a savings-and-loan company. As personalities go, there wasn't a dull one in the bunch. They were all vital, animated, interesting, and articulate. Their lengthy tenure as a committee had allowed them to meld into one of the most harmonious and family-like groups I had ever met anywhere. They were full of happy tales of their experiences, especially when they traveled to other cities to spy out potential ministers who had been recommended to them.

Everybody laughed, for example, at the story of two men from the committee, the manufacturer and the financial adviser, who had gone to a bar in Florida one Saturday night before hearing a minister the next morning. They were sitting at the bar having a beer and listening to the music when an attractive young woman came up to the better-looking of the two and asked if he would like to dance. He demurred but his friend urged him to go ahead, so he did. On the dance floor, the young woman asked if he was from around there. No, he said, he and his friend were from Virginia. What, she asked, were they doing so far from home? "You wouldn't believe me if I told you," he said. "Try me," she responded. So he told her they were members of a pulpit committee looking for a minister.

Suddenly the woman stopped dancing. She stood quite still and looked at his face to see if he was putting her on. Realizing he was telling the truth, she didn't say another word. She simply turned around and walked away, leaving him alone on the dance floor.

Part of my burden in negotiating with any search committee at that time was the responsibility I felt to continue to preach and lecture for other churches and university groups around the country. I had some real presentiments about trying to do this from Lynchburg, which was (and is) a relatively small city in a fairly isolated part of Virginia. While the church was very upscale and sophisticated in some ways, I feared that it would react to a pastor's frequent absences pretty much the way most small-town churches would, perhaps at first with some pride and then, when the novelty waned, with complaints and irritability.

But when I voiced my wariness about this to the committee, they were univocal and insistent that, far from being a problem, this would be an added incentive for their congregation to accept me as their pastor. "You will be part of our mission to the world," is the way one bright, articulate woman on the committee put it. "Yes," said the manufacturer, "this is part of the reason we would like you to be our pastor. You would bring a constant freshness to us and our life as a church by interfacing with the larger world beyond Lynchburg. Our congregation would be thrilled to have you as its representative in other places."

This wasn't the argument that cinched the deal, but it was never far from my mind as I considered the possibility of a call to that church.

There were other issues, of course — the openness or closedness of the congregation on theological and social issues, the church's attitude toward the minister's family life, their receptiveness to new and creative approaches to worship, their stance on missions, their willingness to grant their pastor ample time to study, reflect, and write, their general support of other members of the church staff, and their relationship to larger ecclesiastical bodies and the ecumenical movement itself. But in every instance I received positive assurance that this was an unusually strong and open congregation, ready to follow an intelligent, articulate pastor with a united will and spirit.

On the whole, the committee did know the mind and heart of their church and represent them accurately. They confessed honestly that they had enjoyed a long and fruitful pastorate under Dr. McGukin, a beloved minister who had retired several years earlier and had subsequently passed away, and that their biggest concern since then had been the brevity of their ministers' tenures. One bright young minister from California had stayed only two years and had left to succeed his father as president of a famous prep school. Another, more mature minister had stayed four years and gone to be pastor of a large church in Texas. And a third, extremely well-liked young man had left to become the minister of a large church in Florida.

The problem, they all agreed, was that the church invariably brought in ministers who were in high demand for their abilities and qualifications, and it was hard to keep them when exciting new possibilities opened up to them in other parts of the country. I think they were basically right. The one thing they didn't understand was that all of these ministers had undergone a kind of cultural shock when they came to Lynchburg because of the unique character of the city itself.

A fine old town on the James River, Lynchburg had lost out to nearby Roanoke as a transportation center for southwest Virginia. It was perhaps the largest city in America not serviced by an interstate highway. Consequently, even though it was home to three colleges, plus exclusive little Sweetbriar College only a dozen miles away, it was extremely parochial as similar-sized cities went, and there was a general sense of inbreeding in the community. General Electric had opened a plant there twenty-five years before, and the engineers and their families who had moved there in a considerable invasion were still regarded as "outsiders" by most of the old Lynchburgers. Like the three ministers before me who had left in fairly quick succession, I experienced a certain "standoffishness" in the congregation, a sense that I could never be completely admitted to the inner circle of local feeling and sensibility. People were hospitable to a point—but only to a point. They were incapable of being completely and irrevocably accepting.

Then there was the presence of the Rev. Mr. Jerry Falwell. Lynchburg was his community. He had grown up there. It was his name that had brought the city's name to the consciousness of a nation that had been largely unaware of it. Falwell's Thomas Road Baptist Church, which he had started and grown from a handful of supporters some twenty years before, was either the heart that made the city beat or, if you were of the other persuasion, a great tumor growing on the vital organs of a fine old community. It lay on the opposite side of the city from First Presbyterian

Church and drew its strength largely from the blue-collar constituents of the city, while First Presbyterian was the mainstay of the more elite elements — the doctors, attorneys, business executives, and teachers. But there was no mistaking who the big dog was. As the third largest employer in the city (after G.E. and Babcock-Wilcox, the nuclear power company), Falwell's Thomas Road Baptist Church/ Old-Time Gospel Hour/ Moral Majority/ Liberty University was revered by the town's business leaders and the only daily paper, the Lynchburg *News and Advance*. This created a real schizophrenia in the community. Even many of the townspeople who couldn't stand Falwell's blustering form of Christianity were loath to speak against him, because to do so would have seemed grossly disloyal to the town's most famous son. Consequently, most pastors in the city's hundred-and-fifty or so churches maintained a discreet silence about their noisy, much-publicized neighbor. He was a Goliath in a city of quavering Israelites.

When I questioned the search committee at First Presbyterian Church about Falwell's ministry and its effect on the life and work of their own church, they were essentially dismissive. They had no problem coexisting with him, they said. They disagreed with his theology, if not his politics, but he stayed on his side of town and they stayed on theirs. They weren't competing for the same minds and hearts. We are all working for the kingdom of God, they suggested, only in different ways.

What they didn't know, as I soon realized after going there, was the degree of financial involvement a number of First Presbyterian's members had in Falwell's empire. A couple of years before I met the committee, Falwell's organization had begun to default on bonds that had come due, mostly held by financially inexperienced persons who listened to his radio and TV programs and were eager to invest in a growing religious establishment like his. Falwell had originally promised them huge interest rates on their money, which he said was going to be "used for the Lord." Then, when the bonds became due, his organization wrote to the holders saying that they were experiencing unexpectedly hard times and could pay only a fraction of the face value of the bonds. If the holders would accept the marked-down value, they would be paid. Otherwise they would receive nothing. The government's fraud department brought the case before a Lynchburg judge, who in turn appointed a three-man board of overseers to administer Falwell's financial dealings for a specified period of time. The overseers restructured the organization's debt, repaying bondholders a portion of what they had invested by floating new bonds at very high rates of interest. These were gobbled up by Lynchburg businessmen eager to make a killing. So when I inadvertently challenged the Old-Time Gospel Hour for its opportunistic theology and rapaciousness—I have told this story in *Ten Things I Learned Wrong from a Conservative Church*—several prominent members of my congregation became very uncomfortable. "Don't bulldoze the money tree!" one of them admonished me.

I did continue to speak in other venues after going to Lynchburg, and even made a point, when I did, of letting the congregation know where I was representing them. It soon became obvious, though, that the search committee had misjudged people's reactions to this or had simply been too eager to allay my own fear that my freedom to travel would not be greeted by the same alacrity expressed by the committee members. In my second year at the church, my secretary came into my office with a worried face and told me that one of the members of the now-defunct search committee—the financial adviser—had come to her and asked for a schedule of all the speaking engagements I had fulfilled since arriving at the church. He and another member of the committee—the manufacturer—were clearly out to get me, she said.

"Give them the schedule," I said, "but let me see it first."

When she gave it to me, I spent a few moments adding up all the days I had been away. Then I added to this sum all the days of vacation and study leave I had taken. The total came to less than the amount of my stated vacation time. Armed with this information, I went into a session meeting, at which I am sure the two men were prepared to raise the issue of my being away so much, and broached the matter before they had an opportunity.

There had been some scheming going on behind the scenes, I said, over an apparent discomfort with the amount of time I had spent away from the church on speaking engagements. I then reminded the session of the amount of time I had been promised for vacation and study-leave purposes and pointed out that my combined time away for both speaking engagements and vacation and study leave was less than I had been offered in my contract. I did not like to think that my work was occasioning consternation, I said, and therefore I was going to absent myself from the meeting for thirty minutes while they were free to discuss the matter. At the end of that time, I would return. If they were happy for me to continue as their pastor, with no further dissension about my times away, then we would forget about the matter and never revisit it. If, on the other hand, they were dissatisfied with my work or the amount of time I was spending away, they could say so and I would give them my resignation that very evening.

I was out of the room only ten minutes when one of the elders came to get me and asked me to return. The session stood to its feet and gave me a round of applause, after which one of them voiced a brief apology, thanked me for my openness about the matter, and suggested that we get on with the business of the agenda.

I tell this story to illustrate the way even the sentiments of members of a search committee themselves may change once a new pastor has been wooed and secured for a church. Was the situation misstated by the member who said so enthusiastically that they wanted me to be their outreach to other congregations and other venues? I'm not sure. At the time, I think it was an accurate gauge of the people's sentiments, and there were always some members of that church who were actually proud that their minister was invited to speak in other places. But the fact that it was two men from the search committee who eventually decided that I was away too much suggests that there is always a certain volatility about these matters and the minister who is being courted should not place too much stock in what he or she is told about an entire church's willingness to endorse a certain policy or way of thinking.

On the whole, the search committee from the First Presbyterian Church of Lynchburg was one of the best I ever met, and was most truly in touch with the nature of their congregation and its sentiments. Part of the reason for this is that they represented a very cohesive congregation, one that was unified by geography and demographics as well as by social and political ethos. But it is also a tribute to those remarkable people elected by the congregation to represent them, who took their job very seriously and worked long and patiently to identify and call a pastor whom they believed to be God's own choice for their church. There were no big, ugly surprises in store for us when we moved to Lynchburg. The members of the search committee, moreover, became a team of supporters to aid the new minister and his family for a full year after we arrived in their community.

When we had to leave our furniture behind until our home in Nashville was sold, they found temporary furniture and had it sitting in our new house when we arrived. They brought us casseroles, invited us to lunches and dinners, and helped us with logistical problems as they arose. They prayed for our family as we took up our new roles among them and went out of their way to make us feel welcome.

There was no way they could have anticipated the bad chemistry that would arise between Mr. Falwell and their new minister, or foreseen the possible clash that would occur because a lot of members of their congregation were financially invested in the Old-Time Gospel Hour. Nor could most of them have imagined that two of their own members might become umbrageous about the minister's spending more time than they thought he should preaching and lecturing in other parts of the country. They were a good and thoughtful committee—an exemplary committee, in fact—and I mention the things I recall here only to illustrate the fact that even with the best of search groups there are likely to occur misunderstandings and disappointments because no committee is able to be 100 percent perfect in anticipating the things it needs to share with a potential minister.

༅

Because the Lynchburg committee was so good, I was not really prepared for the misunderstandings and disappointments I would experience from the exuberant promises and projections of the Committee of Eleven, as it was called, from the First Congregational Church of Los Angeles. Actually, this was the second Committee of Eleven I had dealt with at the First Congregational Church, because I had met with the first during the same months when I was talking with the search committee of the First Presbyterian Church in Lynchburg. I had been attracted to the big old Los Angeles church the first time around, and might easily have gone there then. But as I prayed about the two churches and their needs, and humbly acknowledged my own inadequacies as a big-steeple pastor coming off of fifteen years' service as a professor in a divinity school, I felt that God was directing my steps to Virginia and not to the bright lights and rarefied atmosphere of Hollywood and greater Los Angeles.

"OK," the chairman of the search committee in Los Angeles said, "we'll hire an older minister and when he retires we're going to make another pass at you." They were as good as his word. Six years later, when Dr. Donald Ward announced his resignation from the First Congregational Church of L.A., I had a phone call that very day. "How about it?" the voice on the other end of the line said. "Are you ready now to come to L.A.?"

I didn't say yes immediately. I did what any sensible pastor would do, I flew to Los Angeles with my wife and we went through several days of conferences with the members of the new Committee of Eleven. We talked about everything—the temper of the congregation, their budget, the big school that was part of the church's presence, Dr. Ward's ministry, where the church saw itself going in the near future, how the city around the church property was changing, and, of course, what they would expect of me as their minister. The thing that impressed me most was the high level of enthusiasm in the committee. The church had been through some rocky years since the retirement of a long-tenured minister several years earlier. Now it appeared to be stable again, and poised for growth. There were a thousand people, I was told, perhaps even two thousand, who had dropped out of First Church's life because of disenchantment with this or that minister and his inability to command their loyalties. With my coming, all these people would come back to the church at once, and would fuel our ascent to new levels of growth, excitement, and service. There was a television executive on the search committee this time. "We'll go on TV," they all said, "and you'll have Los Angeles at your feet! This church is ready for a renascence!"

They really believed this. In their hope and dreaming, they had convinced themselves that this was the way it would be. There would be citywide hoopla about their new minister, the absentees would return, life would beget life, programs would expand, money would pour in, mission consciousness would rise, God would make a new and lasting impact on the City of Angels! The congregation, which had for years proven contentious and quarrelsome, would be drawn together and react in an unprecedented kind of harmony . . .

They wished.

It was all a pipe dream. The church had been a great church in its day. There was no doubt about that. It had a magnificent sanctuary and church plant that covered the equivalent of a couple of city blocks. Its organ was one of the largest in the world, and the annual concert series brought SRO crowds of music lovers to the church. The yearly Los Angeles Bach Festival, under the supervision of Dr. Thomas Somerville, the great choral director who was minister of music at the church, brought thousands of people together to celebrate Christendom's finest composer. The church's holiday services were renowned for their pageantry and glory. Their school, designed to serve everyone, regardless of race or wealth, produced more National Merit Scholars than any school in the United States. The church owned a 270-acre camp at Big Bear, in the mountains east of L.A., where many famous movies and TV series, such as *Lassie, Sergeant Preston,* and *Bonanza,* were filmed. It also owned a cemetery and several apartment buildings. Its endowment was so large that the giving of the congregation was shamelessly low. It had a sense of class in almost everything it did, and proudly billed itself as "the oldest Protestant congregation in Los Angeles" and "the flagship church of the National Association of Congregational Christian Churches."

But—and here the dash ought to go on for several lines—the church was really an old cadaver hoping for resuscitation.

When I had been there six weeks, I kept wondering where the big crowds of disaffected people were who were supposed to return after I arrived on the scene. "I think we ought to clean the rolls," I said to the board of trustees, "so we can see exactly how many members we are actually working with." Nobody said anything at the meeting, but afterward one well-meaning little man informed me that an associate pastor had been fired two years ago precisely because he wanted to prune the rolls and know where everybody was.

OK, I thought, there's more than one way to skin a cat, even an ecclesiastical cat. So I attacked another problem, the lack of emphasis on stewardship, as a way of getting at the one about the membership. The church had not had a pledge drive since anybody could remember, so I talked up the matter and got the board of trustees to agree to a plan. We created a phone bank of twenty-five phones, all manned by carefully selected volunteers, and every evening for a week these volunteers sat at their posts telephoning our members and recording the results. If a phone had been disconnected or could not be reached for any other reason, the volunteer immediately addressed an envelope to the member explaining our pledge drive and asking the member to help us update our records. These letters were all mailed with first-class postage so that we would receive them back if they were undeliverable for any reason. They were also keyed to come back to the volunteers who sent them, so that they would be in charge of their section of the church roll.

After a few days, the letters became coming back in big mail sacks. Some had the word "deceased" written across them. Others said "moved." On many, the post office had used a rubber stamp to inform us that they were simply "undeliverable."

It would be hard to describe the shock this sent through the congregation. It was like getting a letter from the bank saying that all the money we thought we had in our account had disappeared. Here was an old congregation that had once registered five thousand people in its membership. They assured me when I went there that they had twenty-five hundred or three thousand. Now we could locate fewer than eight hundred of these members. Many, it was obvious, had passed on. Others had drifted away—from the neighborhood, from the church, even from Los Angeles. A sense of unreality set in, like the sense one gets when a loved one has died. They couldn't believe it. Even worse, many couldn't accept it. The information had to be erroneous, they thought. The church was still a strong, vital old institution.

OK, I said, now we're dealing with the way things are. No point in crying over spilled milk. Move on to a more proactive stage. It's time, I said, to begin our TV ministry. TV had proven very effective in cities like Los Angeles and New York. Not to bring money into the church's coffers—that was for the evangelistic salesmen like Falwell and Pat Robertson and Jim Bakker—but to feed people's need for images of church and worship and personal devotion. When the people who lived in apartment buildings saw these programs, they often decided to come calling and see what the churches were like in person.

Sorry, said the financial moguls on the board of trustees, there isn't any money for that. TV is too expensive. Our funds are all invested. We can't afford to take any risks—at least none to the tune of the hundreds of thousands of dollars a good TV ministry would cost.

In the end, we had to be content with some one-minute radio spots played on key stations in the L.A. basin during the morning and after-noon commute hours. A former director of such creations oversaw the practical side of things, I wrote and recorded the messages, we underlaid them with a catchy theme tune my wife Anne wrote, and the spots were aired. They brought several new members to the church, and created a slight buzz in the congregation that something was changing. But it was nothing of the magnitude that the TV ministry originally promised by the search committee would have achieved. Not by a long shot.

The camp in the mountains was a disappointment. So was the school. The camp wasn't being utilized for the church membership at all, but was contracted out most of the time to other churches in the area. And the church's ties with the school had been severed before I arrived on the spot so that the church had almost no leverage at all with the students and their parents to attend services or have anything to do with the church except enjoy its largesse in providing an excellent education at an incredibly low cost.

I don't think the members of the Committee of Eleven knew they were hustling me when they told me all the things the church had going for it. They actually believed the propaganda that had been circulating for years about that grand old church. Like other church members, they read the beautiful *Light on a Gothic Tower*, which was a history of the first hundred years of the congregation illustrated with photographs of the great minis-ters and the progression of buildings from the original to the present one modeled on Magdalen College at Oxford, and assumed that all the encomiums about the church were true. They wanted a church fit for Camelot, and that was the one they imagined they had. So when they introduced potential ministers to their situation, it was bound to have a lot of blarney in it. Or baloney.

I tried to help them to see themselves more clearly and stop living in a dream world. They didn't have three thousand members. They weren't making a sensible use of the fabulous property they owned in the mountains, so that it was bleeding them dry without giving anything back to them as a congregation. Their aging congregation was dwindling, and so were their resources, which, abnormally large as they were, would not last forever. Unfortunately, the minister who succeeded me was a dreamer too, and he was always full of grandiose plans that didn't mesh with the harsh realities of a changing neighborhood and a declining church. At his urging, they spent money as if it would go out of style tomorrow, and when he left they were a lot poorer and not a whit closer to becoming the great old congregation of their distant memory.

But did that stop the next Committee of Eleven from seeing everything through rose-colored glasses and giving the next set of candidates their enthusiastic spiel about what a promising future they had? Not a bit. I couldn't believe it when I saw their ad for a new minister in The *Christian Century*:

> The Search is ON
> for a Senior Minister:
> Vibrant Metropolitan Church
> Celebrating 136 Years of Continuous Worship
> Magnificent Gothic Cathedral and Chapels
> Historic Music Programs and the Great Organs
> A Year-Round Camp with 270 Acres and Lake
> Private School, Preschool-12, College Prep

When I read this glowing masterpiece of a come-on, I thought of a joke about the man who stopped to visit with an old Vermont farmer and said, "Hey, I heard the good news about your son." "And what would that be?" asked the farmer warily. "That he won fifty thousand dollars," said the man. The farmer shifted his cud of tobacco from one side of his mouth to the other, spat a big wad of juice against the roots of a tree, wiped his mouth, and said, "Wal, you're mostly right. 'Twarn't my son, 'twar my nephew. 'Twarn't fifty thousand, 'twar five thousand. Didn't win it, he lost it."

There was no way the church was "vibrant." A friend told me that on the last Mother's Day, which used to be a big-attendance Sunday, there were only sixty-five people in a sanctuary that seats more than sixteen hundred. "Decrepit" would have been a more accurate word. The cathedral and chapels were still intact, but they were in ever greater need of repair. An earthquake had shifted the four corner-points of the Gothic tower, breaking the metal bars that braced them in place, so that one was sitting precariously off the edge of its base. It had cost forty thousand dollars to bring in a huge crane and remove all four. They were presently stored in the church's cemetery, without any prospect of replacement. The music programs had been reduced to the bare essentials, and a new organist was hired at half the salary being paid to the great Fred Swann before he retired. The camp was still being used by everyone but First Congregational Church, and still represented an enormous drain on the church's budget. And the school, which was declining in quality, was still not an instrument of the church's outreach for new members and supporters. It was all a great chimera, a huge shimmering dream that refuses to go away as long as there is one parishioner alive who remembers the church in its actual heyday.

One of my good friends was on the Committee of Eleven's short list as they sought a new minister. He asked me to be honest and tell him the problems the church was facing. I told him, no holds barred, and suggested questions he might ask the committee to get at the real truth of the matter. He used e-mail a lot, but when he asked his questions he never got real answers to them. Even when he went to visit them he came away with a sense of unreality, as if they were playing at their task of finding a minister and expected God's own representative to somehow drop out of the clouds and into their arms.

"The only viable reason for going as minister of that church," I told my friend, "is if you honestly feel that God is calling you to do it. Otherwise you should avoid it like the plague."

Los Angeles would be an exciting experience, I said, and he would love a lot of the people he would meet in the church and out of it. But the church itself, with its grandiose dreams that could never be fulfilled, would be bound to disappoint him. As one deacon who was at the church when I was the minister there said, "The problem with life-support systems like the one our endowment gives us is that the patient can be dead a long time before anybody knows it." My friend was in a good situation where he was and had the promise of an even better appointment in the future. He thought it over, talked with his wife, and prayed about it. In the end, he wrote the Committee of Eleven a Dear John and declined to pursue the matter any farther. He felt that the committee members were all high on smog fumes and hadn't an inkling of an idea about what their church was really like.

༄

I haven't meant to bad-mouth pastoral search committees or to suggest that they are all nefarious people. On the contrary, most people who serve on these committees are among the best members in their churches, and, if they tend to overstate the virtues of the churches, it is because they naturally look at their situations in the brightest terms possible. They are almost always pleasant and personable. They wouldn't be selected to represent the congregation if they weren't. They aren't like Alexander Woollcott, the writer, who was so unattractive as a college student that his fellow fraternity members sent him to sit on the front porch of a rival fraternity during pledge week. They are in many cases the nicest and sweetest people in their church.

The point is that they often can and do give misinformation to prospective ministers about the congregations and communities they represent. They obviously love their churches or they wouldn't devote a year or more of all their spare time — and some that isn't so spare — to the task of finding a new pastor. And, as Shakespeare said, love is blind. They willfully cease to see a lot of the warts and wrinkles on their favorite church. They overlook the fact that the last minister left in anger and disappointment, and don't say much about how inhospitable he found many of the strongest members of his boards and committees. They purposefully put the best face on the church's economic situation, and always insist that no matter how well people have given in the past, it is nothing in comparison with what they will do when they get a new minister to lead them. They praise the local schools, commend the shops, exhibit the best restaurants, and make the place sound like a minor paradise. They don't set out at first to prevaricate about the situation as some people might see it. That sense of boosterism just creeps in as they go along. They gradually come to be a sort of mini-Chamber of Commerce for the church and the community as well, and the prospective pastor, assuming that good Christian people always tell the truth, even if they do it in love, is being naturally hoodwinked for Jesus without any evil intended.

My rule for listening to a search committee, which I employed the last time Anne and I talked with one representing a congregation in New York City, is to smile, divide everything they say by half, subtract another twenty percent, multiply by .17$\frac{1}{2}$, and then chew the remainder cautiously, being careful not to swallow anything. I don't say this in derision or with any malice whatsoever. It is simply a fact of life that search committees, for all their good intentions, never see things realistically and therefore are incapable of providing potential ministers with the truth they think they need in order to make a sound decision. Forewarned is forearmed. As I told my friend who was talking with my old church in Los Angeles, the only real reason for going to a church that is represented by one of these whitewashing, double-talking committees is that God wants you to do it. If he wants it, you've got to do it. Otherwise, you're completely on your own. And either way it's a leap off a cliff!

Five

Preaching to the Same Congregation Sunday after Sunday Is Extremely Hard Work!

Preaching is, provided the sermons are theologically sound, intellectually interesting, and full of truly human content, as opposed to being full of religious jargon and rhetorical emptiness, extremely hard work. *Incredibly* hard work.

I had no idea, when I began my trek in ministry. Then, I assumed that the time would come when sermons would simply well up out of my expansive knowledge of the faith and understanding of people, those hidden springs of basic wisdom. The assumption was not challenged by my professors in seminary—not even my homiletics professor, who surely knew what hard work his own preaching was. George Buttrick's *Sermons Preached in a University Church*—Buttrick was preacher to Harvard University—was surely one of the five or ten best volumes of sermons published in the twentieth century. But Buttrick never said what mind-sweating, backbreaking work it was to produce such a book.

The difficult part, of course, is doing it while performing as a juggler and a funambulist, or tightrope walker. The minister has dozens, even hundreds, of other tasks during any given week—unless he or she has an enviable post like the one Fosdick had at Riverside Church in New York, where he was only the preaching minister and nothing else—and there are weeks when those other tasks simply inundate the time for preparation.

I had an e-mail just this week from my friend Robert Hundley, a fine United Methodist preacher in Michigan. An earlier e-mail had expressed joy at having cleared a couple of days on his calendar to prepare his Easter sermon, surely one of the hardest of the year to bring off with the kind of éclat it clearly deserves. This one bemoaned the fact that Bob had suddenly had two funerals thrust into his week's work—entailing visits to the relatives, arranging the services, preparing remarks, doing the gravesides, and calling on the relatives again after they were over—and had to put his Easter sermon into EM, or emergency mode, meaning whenever he could find the time to work on it.

Many ministers, given the Herculean job of preparing truly worthy sermons each week, simply give up early and get in the habit of rattling off inane comments with a preassigned title for the bulletin or—heavens, don't tell anybody!—borrowing other people's work. The load at my old parish in Los Angeles was so heavy that the board of trustees finally employed a ghostwriter to compose the sermons my successor preached— a ghostwriter who, he claimed, had the same social and theological mindset that he had, which was supposed to make it OK, the way a president's having a speechwriter is OK.

"You shall know the truth," said Jesus, "and the truth will make you free." I loved that verse when I was a young Christian just starting on my life's trajectory. It was two promises in one, that knowing the truth is possible and that when one knows it one is free regardless of his or her external circumstances. It's really very Zenlike, having to do with an untrammeled spirit in the midst of a contentious, difficult world. When I got to divinity school and saw the statue of John Harvard, serenely bronze, in Harvard

Yard. I also liked it that the motto on the base of the statue said "Veritas," the Latin word for truth. Again it was the promise of something wonderful to come: I was on a journey toward the truth, and once I got there my life would assume an incredible new dimension.

Throughout my career as a minister, I struggled to discover and then speak the truth. I disdained sermons that didn't have any uncovered truth in them, that merely repeated what everybody already knew, shoving it around like a tug-of-war in the snow without making tracks in a particular direction. I think this was the big romance of preaching for me. Every sermon was like a treasure hunt, and when I got into the pulpit on Sunday morning it was in order to hold up the treasure and say "Here it is!" Or, more accurately, it was in order to recreate for my hearers the journey I had made to get to the particular truth enshrined in the sermon, so that they could follow the way with me and have the thrill of stumbling upon the truth for themselves. That moment in a sermon, which comes about five minutes from the end and is roughly equal to the denouement in a play or a novel, where everything becomes resolved and the listener or hearer suddenly sees the light shining through it, illuminating everything, has for me always been one of the choicest moments of a lifetime. And the greater the truth at the kernel of the sermon, the richer and more unforgettable the moment.

e-∂

But I am a lot older and wiser now, and I know a secret about preaching that I didn't know earlier. That secret is that most people who come to church couldn't care less about following the clues in a sermon until they actually come upon the truth for themselves. In fact, most people actively dislike having to search for the truth and would be totally flustered if they happened upon it. Finding the truth changes us. Every bit of it that we discover makes different persons of us. And most people don't want to be changed. What did the poet say, "Most people would rather die than be changed"?

In other words, there is not much premium in the church on real preaching, preaching that seeks to uncover the truth and reveal it to people. People prefer to enjoy instead the repetition of the half-truths they already know, cosmeticized and represented in a way that they find entertaining and nonthreatening. Nuggets of wisdom they have handled until they fairly gleam from the fondling.

Entertainment is a key word in modern culture. Aldous Huxley anticipated it way back in 1932 when he published *Brave New World*, his novel in which people no longer care about ideas—Shakespeare and the Bible have been locked away in a safe—but relax with drugs and "feelavision," their version of virtual-reality TV. Now, in many parts of the world, his predictions have come true and everything in the culture is directed toward escape and entertainment. Even so-called "reality TV" has become a symbol of our passion for being enthralled. People vie for survival on a desert island by passing a number of tests devised by twenty-five-year-old studio executives sitting with their feet on their desks in an air-conditioned boardroom in Santa Monica. The tests fabricate the kind of ordeals a modern Robinson Crusoe might face on a coral reef in the South Pacific. The safety net is always there—nobody ever gets killed. But crisis management in the wilderness has been turned into a form of voyeurism for twenty-first-century couch potatoes who wouldn't know the first thing to do in a real wilderness.

In the end, we lose our sense of what is real and what isn't. Where do life's actual crises end and the imitation ones take over, or vice versa? Are we so jaded with life, so protected from the hard edges of the survival-of-the-species thing, that we have to manufacture facsimile dangers in order to trick our adrenaline and experience a thrill?

Maybe bungee jumping will one day be regarded by anthropologists as a symbol of our culture—the contrived near-death experience in which idle people hurl themselves off bridges or towers and plunge toward extinction thirty-two feet per second in order to *feel* something in this age of deadened sensibilities. What is wrong with a society that is so soft and has it so easy that it must create false security threats in order to jump-start its sense of excitement? Whatever happened to facing death the way Hemingway did, in wars and bullfights, or the way missionary doctors do, spending their vacations in Africa treating AIDS victims and vaccinating bloated-bellied children for polio and typhoid fever?

But that's all a sermon in itself. We're talking here about the fact that people who chill out on entertainment all the time don't come to church to be faced with the great existential dilemmas of real faith and commitment. They come to be entertained some more, to have the preacher continue the charade they're living in the rest of their lives. In other words, they come to church to play-act at being Christian, not actually to follow Jesus. They want the minister's sermon to be a seamless extension of their daily patterns, something that lets them posture at church the way they've been posturing all week at home and school and the marketplace.

Woe to the minister who dares to interrupt their patterns, who calls their daily lives into question by suggesting that they haven't been living at all, not in any primeval, epochal sense, but have been tiptoeing through meadows of artificial flowers and mechanical bumblebees! He or she is spotted at once as that most dangerous of creatures in the world of entertainment, a spoil-sport radical, a reality-monger of the worst kind. All the antennae go on full alert! The safeguards are triggered and set in motion. The floaters—the nomadic Christians who drift from church to church without ever settling—simply waft away to other venues where the sermons are less threatening, while the home guard, the embedded entertainment freaks, begin their networked campaign to unseat the pastor and send him or her packing. Nobody wants rebels in paradise, disturbers of the status quo.

Maybe this explains why so many pastors relax early in their careers into the habit of preaching unimportant sermons—bits of fluff-and-stuff just sufficiently glittering with current religious catchwords to sound appropriately pious but still seriously nonthreatening to anybody's presently assumed notions of what constitutes either a religious lifestyle or a respectable Christian congregation. They learn a notable truth, that cloning the sermons of certain "successful" pastors—albeit that they are probably not in favor of biological cloning!—is the safest path for them as the paid leaders of the congregation and the way for them to have their cake and eat it too, without leaving a trail of telltale crumbs that might identify them as radical thinkers or secret corrupters.

It is, of course, one way of dealing with the extreme busyness of the average pastor's existence. If pastors can evade the requirement of a weekly sermon forged on the flatiron of the minister's own knowledge of biblical faith and exposure to the daily crises and joys of the congregation, then they're already one leg up on their killer schedules and have more breathing room for the multifold duties of their calling. It's an easy way out, to be sure. Lowering one's self-expectations because the congregation only wants to be entertained, not challenged by the great demands of historical Christianity, is basically as much a cop-out as that of a security guard who neglects his duties because he trusts the sophisticated alarm system and knows that he wouldn't be any match for a gang of intruders anyway.

What did God say to the prophet Ezekiel? "Mortal, I have made you a sentinel for the house of Israel"—the old KJV called it a "watchman"— "whenever you hear a word from my mouth, you shall give them warning from me" (Ezekiel 3:17). Sounds pretty serious, doesn't it? But we preachers are clever at defusing such orders.

∽

Surely it will not be surprising to most readers that there are beaucoup homiletical services out there today ready to provide an almost infinite number of cloned sermons for pastors who haven't time to write their own or are afraid to write their own, lest they prove infected by some germ of originality that might upset the whole entertainment cycle for their congregations. They exist in every shade and format, mirroring all those popular magazines with names like *People, Us, In Touch,* and *Entertainment*—different mastheads for the same boring stream-of-unconsciousness stuff in New York and Tinsel Town.

One of the most adventurous (defining "adventure" as what happens in a theme park) is the multimedia sermon being marketed by several online firms whose credo is that if people want entertainment when they come to church, why not give it to them in 3-D, by treating them to film clips, dramatic interludes, Thomas Kinkade-ish pictures, and a potpourri of scriptures, religious music, and brief excerpts from popular books? My wife and I have attended a Methodist church where the pastor subscribes to such sermon helps. There are two big movie screens, one on either side of the chancel, and a computer setup at the back of the sanctuary manned by an engineer with a script and twin projectors. The pastor "talks" his way through part of the sermon, then holds up his bulletin as a cue to the engineer to flip on the first multimedia aid. A colorful scene appears on the screens, with a scripture text printed on it. The minister reads the text aloud. He goes on with his sermon. When he comes to another bullet on his script, he lifts his bulletin again, and presto, there is a two-minute clip from some saccharine old religious movie. And so it goes for the entire sermon. There is a recognizable similarity between the pacing of the sermon, with all its multimedia facets, and the pacing of a TV program and its commercial interruptions. Nobody's intellect is challenged too much. In fact, it isn't challenged at all. Nobody has a problem with ADS—"attention deficit for sermons"— because there are so many shifts during the fifteen or eighteen minutes of the sermon that there is never time to get bored. Unless, that is, one finds the whole process somewhat tedious and devoid of meaning.

The thing I've noted, too, is that these canned sermon experiences— I'm not sure they can really be called sermons—invariably include references or quotations from the most popular Christian writers featured in the local Christian bookstore. Max Lucado. Philip Yancey. Charles Stanley. Franklin Graham or his sister Anne Lotz. Joyce Meyer. It's all a package deal. There is an "approved" Christianity out there on the market these days, and that is what is safe for all the pastors to allude to. If they go afield and mention writers or thinkers not on the accepted list—say, Matthew Fox or Karen Armstrong or Thomas Moore or Kathleen Norris—they are liable to provoke a reaction from someone in the congregation who read one of those writers and found him or her aberrant in orthodoxy.

It is always safer, in any generation, to follow the crowd. That way the preachers don't get into hot water. Their position is always defensible. Never mind that Jesus was a radical and provoked trouble everywhere he went, pricking people's favorite balloons and upsetting their applecarts. If the minister doesn't want any trouble, and doesn't want to be looking for a new job on Monday morning, then it is best to stick with the "in folks" on Sunday and allude only to the authors, works, and ideas that have already been plastered with a kosher sticker.

There is, I fear, a greater consent to uniformity in the church today than there has been since the Middle Ages, before the febrile Reformation that encouraged the kind of diversity of opinion that gave birth to dozens of Christian denominations. It exists as an unspoken code in our churches, our denominations, and our publishing houses. Some Christian publishers actually guard their books and magazines with near-fanaticism, avoiding any statements or references that might signal a divergence from the generally accepted orthodoxy. Just as there is a political correctness in public utterances and a spirit of conformity in public life generally, there is a noticeable fear in our churches of being different from everybody else, of saying anything radical or heterodox and thus appearing aberrant. It conveys a sense of unreality about our common life as Christians, an atmosphere of distrust and anxiety that belies the dynamic and exciting gospel at the very heart of our joint endeavor.

Many pastors, aware of the rush to judgment among their parishioners, now sanitize their sermons to the point of absolute blandness. It is in my opinion a great failing of the pulpit today that almost every minister sounds identical to every other minister. The Christian experience in America is being programmed so that future generations of converts will know only a monolithic version of the faith and miss the rich, polychromatic texture of Christianity through the ages. What must Jesus think of preaching—he who unfailingly uttered such incredible worth, and with such unfaltering courage?

༄

When I think of the subject of real courage in preaching, I often think of Robert Bolt's play about Thomas More, *A Man for All Seasons*. More, it will be recalled, was King Henry VIII's archbishop, whom Henry ordered to be executed for not supporting his wish to divorce his queen. Everyone in the audience knows the story, of course, so anticipates More's ending from the beginning of the play. But Bolt makes the conflict absorbing until the very moment of More's execution, when a large guillotine is assembled on the stage and he is made to kneel before it, his head in the half-circle of stock. Suddenly the lights go out and there is the sound, first, of the giant blade falling—*plonking!*— onto something. Then there is the sound of a cabbage— or a head—dropping into a large wicker basket. Even in its anticipation, the audience is invariably stunned at this.

There is a moment of absolute silence.

And then the little Everyman character who has been the interlocutor at several stages of the play, explaining things to the audience about historical details that would have been difficult to encompass in the drama itself, comes bounding out of the darkness to speak. In the version of the play I saw, in London, he was a rotund little figure dressed in a black leotard and looking somewhat comical, like the fool in a royal court. "I'm breathing," he says, gulping in some air. "Are you?" He looks around. "It isn't hard," he says. "Just don't make trouble"—an allusion to More's problem. "Or, if you do, make the kind that's expected!"

Make the kind that's expected. There is a lot of wisdom in that remark. Some kinds of trouble are expected, even from a preacher. Attacks on immorality. Chiding about an ungenerous attitude. Reminders of a church's duty to the poor. Warnings about straying from positions of orthodoxy. Rants against sin-in-general—"God is holy and all flesh is wicked." Accusations that certain ideas are unbiblical. These sorts of trouble have been identified with the parson's persona at least since Chaucer's day. They go with the territory and most people don't take them very seriously.

But *unexpected* kinds of trouble are a different matter altogether. Attacks on church officers for behaving in less than Christian fashion. Taking part in a demonstration for racial or social equality. Insisting on the rights of women or gays. Criticizing the government when it behaves irresponsibly toward other nations or its own constituency. Siding with the minority in a big church battle. Repudiating contemporary Christianity for its lack of Christian sensibility. Standing up for religious and social pariahs. Laughing at the threats of important congregational leaders.

I have never known a minister to get fired or even scolded for making the kind of trouble that everybody expected. But I have never known one who didn't get fired or scolded or grievously treated for making the kind that nobody expected. Maybe we ought to call it More's Law.

Jesus, according to the Jews, spoke "as one having authority, not as the scribes and Pharisees," because he rejected the group-think of his day. The Jewish leaders rightly pegged him for a radical, because he devoted his ministry to overthrowing the tyranny of a religious system that had covered his country like a malignant tumor and disdained the search for any new truth. Whatever its beginnings, that system, like any system that is ultimately successful and controlling, became false and corrupt because it was no longer interested in seeking new ways of being open to God's Spirit. Assuming that it possessed the truth, it became demonic in its defense of error. From the beginning of his ministry in the desert, Jesus was destined to die, if not at the hands of the Romans then at the hands of his countrymen who could not bear to have their supremacy challenged. We often forget the bravery of this prophetic man as he traveled from town to town, inventing parables and saying things that would not go down well with the authorities.

It is a brave preacher today who opts to speak from his or her own heart instead of merely repeating what the in-crowd is saying. There are enormous personal pressures on ministers to conform to the generally accepted version of Christianity and not raise questions about it. But of what value are preachers who don't seek and then speak the truth, who merely echo what everybody else has agreed is a "correct" version of scriptural ideals and teachings? Perhaps they fulfill a certain social necessity by being spokespersons for the party line. If they don't do it, others will. The church can always raise up popular prophets, ministers who have been coopted to ratify its pronouncements and make them acceptable to a general public.

But is that being faithful to Jesus, who risked his very life to say things that jarred the religious consciousness of his day? Is that what idealistic young men and women who enter the ministry want to spend their lives doing? Or are they simply too naive to resist the wiles of the system until it has swallowed them whole and then spit them out in its own image? There must be many ministers of the church today who are secretly despondent about the way they have sold out to the system, exchanging their souls for a chance to be accepted, recognized, and rewarded. Somewhere in Kierkegaard's journals he speaks of having been the life of a party he attended and then having gone home and immediately wanted to shoot himself. There are surely thousands of such ministers today who have paid a price for fitting in, for getting a church and then keeping it, and now feel like offing themselves, Judaslike, for their betrayal of the genuine way, the genuine truth, and the genuine life.

One of the saddest figures I see in the church is the minister who secretly wants to become a real preacher, a true follower of the Master, and doesn't quite know how. Often this minister admires a prominent dissident in the church and wishes to be like him or her. So he or she begins to preach the dissident's sermons, either in *toto* or somewhat revised. I remember a young minister who came to be pastor of the Presbyterian church in Nashville my wife and I attended. He had the right instincts about suspecting the system and directing people to be more thoughtful in their approach to the faith. But he lacked the courage to step out on his own and say things that came from his own heart. Instead, he repreached the sermons of Carlyle Marney, the noted minister of Myers Park Baptist Church in Charlotte, North Carolina.

I had known Marney for years, and was familiar with many of his sermons. So when this young preacher began reproducing Marney's stuff in the pulpit I noticed it immediately. "OK," I thought, "he recognizes good material when he reads it, and if he wants to replicate Marney's sermons for our little congregation, so be it." But when he told Marney's personal stories as his own—"I turned to this lady on an airplane and said. . ."— that was too much. I lost my last shreds of respect for the man. He might at least have said, "As Carlyle Marney once said . . ."

Obviously many ministers lift other ministers' sermons. Every few months, one reads or hears about some prominent minister who has lost his pulpit because somebody in his congregation discovered that he (I don't recall that it ever happened to a woman) was plagiarizing the works of other ministers. When I moved to Birmingham, it had just happened to the minister of the largest Baptist church in the city. One of his enemies in the church got hold of the sermons he was copying—from a minister in Florida, as I recall—and gave a parallel, side-by-side account of the originals and this minister's "reworked" versions to the local papers, which actually published them. It was an unforgivably embarrassing thing to do. The minister apologized and described the enormous pressures he was under—mostly psychological pressures from his warfare with some of the church leaders, which he said had rendered him unable to write his own sermons even though he was a very capable craftsman.

A similar thing happened recently to a minister at National City Christian Church in Washington, D.C., who had been plagiarizing sermons he found on the internet from two or three prominent preachers. His life was a runaway wagon on a downhill grade, he said, and he clutched at these sermons by his *confrères* in ministry as acts of desperation. But because he himself was such a prominent preacher, and his church was such a showcase for its denomination (the Disciples of Christ), not even he could live with the aftermath of exposure.

A minister friend in Texas was excited, when he spoke at a convention in that state, to be preaching side-by-side with a well-known New York clergyman. A few weeks later he was visiting New York and went with some friends to hear the distinguished pastor. He couldn't believe it when the minister began to preach—he was hearing the sermon he himself had preached at the convention in Texas! He wanted to duck out a side door after the service, but his friends, who attended that church, insisted that he accompany them through the main door and meet their minister. When the minister saw him, he visibly blanched. But bravely he took the Texas pastor aside and explained: "I have been so busy this week . . . I thought your sermon was one of the best I had ever heard . . . couldn't resist borrowing it . . . please forgive me."

And, of course, one of the most notorious cases in the twentieth century, though one that never appeared in any newspaper, was that of the posthumous publication of the famous Washington preacher Peter Marshall's *Mr. Jones, Meet the Master*. A collection purporting to be some of Marshall's finest sermons, arranged in the semipoetical spacing style he liked to use in the pulpit, the book became a best seller and was read and quoted all over the English-speaking world. Unfortunately, and unbeknown to Marshall's widow, Catherine, who idolized her husband and wrote a best-selling biography of him entitled *A Man Called Peter*, later made into a widely viewed motion picture, Marshall had been in the habit of lifting sermons from some of the most distinguished preachers in both his native Scotland and the United States, reorganizing them for his own delivery style, and preaching them from the pulpit of the New York Avenue Presbyterian Church in Washington, the church that contains the so-called "Lincoln Pew" where President Lincoln sat when he attended services. Several of the real owners of those sermons got together and contacted Mrs. Marshall to tell her that her husband had infringed on their rights, and eventually a settlement was reached and *Mr. Jones, Meet the Master* was quietly withdrawn from circulation. Mercifully, they did not seek public vindication for the infringements.

What can one say about such borrowing? Most ministers are pretty charitable about those who are caught doing it, for they themselves know the temptations. They are often too busy to write decent sermons and would like to plagiarize the sermons of others. Or they lack the talent for writing great sermons and feel that it is better to poach the material of others than it is to have nothing worth saying on their own. It could be pointed out in their behalf that even Shakespeare, unquestionably the greatest writer in the English language or perhaps even in any language in the world, freely borrowed the plots for his finest dramas from the writings of others.

But the tragedy, in my opinion — and I do not think "tragedy" is too strong a word — is that ministers who borrow the sermons of others miss out on the greatest privilege of their professional existence, the opportunity to reflect on their own inimitable journeys of faith, together with what they know about the Bible and people's lives, and to speak words that are truly their own, so that the interface between them and the lives of their congregation becomes a living, thriving, spiritual connection in a world that is increasingly void of such connections. When they take the easy way out, adapting the sermons of others or using materials they have purchased from a homiletical service of some kind, they are cheating themselves of the growth that would come to them over the course of their ministries and mark them as what H. H. Farmer once called "servants of the Word."

How long does it take to write a good sermon? Fosdick once went to church on his vacation and heard one of his own sermons from the mouth of the young cleric. Shaking hands with the man as he left, Fosdick asked how long it had taken him to prepare that sermon. The young minister smiled and said dismissively, "Oh, two or three hours, I guess." "That's funny," said Fosdick. "I'm a lot older and more experienced than you, and it cost me more than twenty hours!"

No one can put a precise figure on the length of time required to produce a serious sermon. I have heard George Buttrick, Ralph Sockman, Paul Scherer, and other great New York preachers say that they needed an hour of study and preparation for every minute spent in the pulpit. Personally, I never had the luxury of that kind of time. But I did try to discipline myself to spend at least two mornings a week in my study at home working on the sermon and prayers for the next Sunday. Sometimes a sermon would come quickly, like a baby ready to be birthed before its arrival time. Other times it would come slowly, in fits and spurts, agonizingly, as if it didn't want to come together at all. But I always treated them as the central task I had to do as a minister. If I didn't, then everything else would have collapsed. The sermons were the linchpins of what I was called to do with my weeks.

I have occasionally been asked how long I have been working on a particular sermon. The answer I once gave actually proved standard for most of them: "All of my life." Because that's what a sermon is, actually — it is the total being and experience of the minister, filtered through a particular biblical text or controlling idea for a specific time of delivery. Sometimes it comes out of the minister's peak experiences, as Abraham Maslow called them — those moments when we soar and all our cylinders are firing with glorious precision. And other times it comes out of his or her depth experiences — the times when we stumble blindly through life, buffeted by the blows of an apparently careless fate and praying desperately for some reprieve. But wherever it comes from, it is part of the minister's own personal life reaching out to communicate with a bunch of other people who are also on a dicey pilgrimage through an often alien and dubious world.

It is indeed a high privilege to be called "minister" or "pastor" and be set aside by ordination to do this, to sift through the ragbag of human experiences and offer hope and support to fellow travelers. We weren't warned it would be so hard and demanding — or that we would be so busy that we might not have time to do it acceptably — but it is a pity to give up the privilege and renounce the benefits.

∽

Okay, so it's hard and they didn't warn us in seminary. So it demands more time than the minister has to give to it — time when we would like to be enjoying our spouses and children, time carved out of often impossible schedules, time stolen from personal needs or pleasures, time barricaded from imperious secretaries or insistent congregations, time derived from hours when we could be sleeping or resting or watching TV. I have never known a minister who was worth his or her salt as the pastor of a congregation who did not spend the requisite time preparing a sermon for Sunday morning (or Saturday, in the case of Adventists) and then devoting his or her utmost to the communication of that sermon. Not a single one.

Of course, not all sermons are equal, any more than all omelettes, watermelons, or hunting dogs are equal. We won't always hit the center of the target, any more than we could do it on an archery range or a firing range. But the consistency with which we make the attempt, the steadfastness with which we hold to our time for study and preparation, will ensure not only that we are faithful to our charge but that we are constantly growing and deepening as ministers of the Word — not the Word as a static, literal transcript of ancient manuscripts, but the Word as a living, breathing, creative Spirit that sweeps us up in its wild flow and continually works at transforming our lives!

There is a delightful little story about Paderewski, the world-famous pianist, that has often inspired me when I was tempted to give up the discipline of my calling. He had just played a concert for Queen Victoria, and she was smitten by the glory of it. "Mr. Paderewski," she exclaimed as she applauded, "you are a genius!" "That may well be, madam," said the pianist, bowing in courtesy. "But before that I was a drudge."

God will not judge us on the size of our talent—whether we can move people like Chrysostom or Spurgeon or Billy Graham—but solely on the basis of our faithfulness to the responsibilities we were given. I would rather produce a sermon that was the offering of my own heart and intellect, a poem of love and illumination from the depth of my own soul, than to be the wealthiest man in the world—even if I wasn't warned that it could be difficult, demanding, and sometimes even dangerous.

Six

There Is a Meanness in Some Church Members that Is Simply Incredible

There's a wonderful story about Professor Inman Johnson, a longtime teacher at Southern Baptist Theological Seminary in Louisville. "Prof" Johnson, as he was known affectionately by students and others, spent most of his career at the seminary supplementing his inadequate salary, as most of the other professors did, by serving as an interim minister for churches seeking pastors.

It was often the case that a pastoral search committee in a church Prof Johnson was serving took a long time in its process because they were so happy to have him in their pulpit instead of some struggling young minister who would inevitably be appointed to the post. One time the process went on and on and on. The years came and went, and people began celebrating Prof Johnson's anniversaries as their supply pastor— the fifth, the seventh, the tenth. Finally, in his thirteenth year as interim minister, one of the deacons in the church, who had become a good friend of Johnson's, said to him, "Prof, you've been here a long time now. Why don't you just become our pastor?"

"Hell," Johnson is said to have responded, "I've seen how you treat your ministers!"

It's hard to figure why congregations of Christians, of all the groups in the world, should be so punishing toward their ministers and their spouses. Maybe it is precisely because it is so surprising that Christian people should behave with anything other than kindness, tolerance, and love—to anybody—that we find it difficult to believe that some of them have actually been known to persecute their pastors and their families.

But it is sadly true.

Maybe there are a few professors of pastoral care in the seminaries who level with their students about this phenomenon, but I didn't have any who did. In fact, I cannot remember a single seminary professor I had in *any* field, although in the course of my studies I attended three different seminaries, who ever said a word about the difficulties we were liable to encounter in any pastorate we assumed upon leaving seminary. Reflecting on this, I attribute it to the fact that most seminary teachers have never spent any time in the trenches before embarking on their professorial careers, and so are blithely unaware of how desperate and bitter are the situations of some local pastors.

I do remember George Buttrick, who taught church administration as well as preaching, making amusing little remarks about the eccentricities of various church members. For example, in commenting on the personalities of some church ushers, he said that sticking a flower in a man's buttonhole and sending him down the middle aisle of a church can alter his personality forever. But even he, who surely bore the marks of a number of duels and free-for-alls in his several congregations, never said a word to prepare us for the hostility and acrimony we were likely to encounter in any church we pastored. So maybe it is part of the gentleman's code or something—not to kiss and tell, or to rat on congregations that are less than charitable toward those who are called to be their spiritual leaders.

But people can be unbelievably grudging and mean to their ministers.

Years ago, I visited a church in San Juan, Puerto Rico, two or three times as a speaker and became lifetime friends with Homer and Lorraine

Thompson, two of the leading laypeople of the congregation. Homer was head of the public relations office of Peat, Marwick, Mitchell, the national accounting firm, and made a handsome salary with which he was quite generous to others. Several years before he retired, he and Lorraine purchased a retirement home in Florida, where they expected to spend the later years of their lives. But when he actually retired and they returned to Florida, they didn't like the house as much as they had when they bought it, so they donated it to the local Methodist church as a parsonage for the church's minister, and with it provided money for the church to refurnish the house. In the congregation's gratitude, they immediately asked Lorraine to serve on the parsonage committee.

"I couldn't believe, when I went with that committee of ladies to look at furniture," said Lorraine, "how niggardly and begrudging some of them were toward the pastor's family. When someone said that a particular easy chair looked lovely and comfortable, another woman said, 'That's too nice for them!' When someone else liked a beautiful lamp, another woman said, 'That's better than any lamp I have in my house.' It was that way about everything. People didn't want their minister and his family to have anything as nice as the things in their own houses!"

More recently, my wife's sister Mary, who attended a church in Oak Ridge, Tennessee, told us the story of a new minister who had been called by the congregation. He and his wife had a severely retarded daughter, and they requested that the parsonage committee, in their usual freshening up of the house after the tenure of the last minister and his family, paint the rooms in different pastel colors so the daughter would have less difficulty telling one room from another. It seemed a simple and reasonable request. But the committee refused to honor it.

"We're not painting our parsonage to suit a new minister and his retarded daughter," some members were reported to have said. "Nobody knows how long they'll be here, and then we'd have to go back and paint it all again."

⌒

This attitude is not widespeard in most congregations. In fact, most ministers I know would testify that fewer than 10 percent of their members ever say cutting things or behave unkindly toward them in any way. Many congregants are generous, loving people and want to make their pastors and their families as happy and comfortable as possible. They welcome them to their churches with open arms, bringing flowers and casseroles and desserts. They pray for their work in the community. They send them little notes of kindness and cheer. They come to love them and receive them with hugs and kisses when they meet at parties or public gatherings.

But sometimes a minister under fire can feel as if the numbers are reversed, and it is 90 percent of the people who are after his or her hide, while only 10 percent behave with decency and civility. There are two reasons for this. One is that the unkindness of the pastor's enemies is often shown in private, so that the majority of people aren't aware of it. And the other is that good, kind, ordinary church members are usually baffled by the ill will shown to their ministers and, not knowing quite how to handle it, normally end by saying or doing nothing to combat it.

When I was a pastor in Lynchburg, Virginia, feuding with Rev. Jerry Falwell over the methods and theology of TV evangelists, I was regularly excoriated in the local newspapers by people who wrote in to say that I was ignorant, prejudiced, heretical, and undoubtedly crazy. But even though I had a large church full of members who I am sure were my friends, many of whose friendship I cherish to this day, not once in my six-year tenure in that congregation did a single one of them write to the newspaper to protest the partisanship of the editor or the inaccuracy with which my attackers pilloried me. Most of them probably thought it was my quarrel and I could take care of myself—which I did, quite adequately. But I would cherish now, all these years later, the memory of at least one church member who agreed with the stance of his or her pastor and leapt to his defense in the public arena.

"When the chips are down," said one pastor friend, "the bad guys come out of the woodwork, and the good guys lie low or slink away, leaving you to fend for yourself. It's just like in politics. They have to live there after you're gone, and they're not about to make enemies of people they want to get along with."

If I were a pastor again, I think I would preach an occasional sermon dramatizing the importance of supporting one's friends and leaders against unmerited criticism. One of them might be about the time Simon Peter drew his sword, in the Garden of Gethsemane, and cut off the ear of the servant of the high priest, who had come with the soldiers to arrest Jesus. Another might be about Joseph of Arimathea, who befriended Jesus to the Sanhedrin and later buried him in his own private tomb. It might even be possible to preach a sermon about the helplessness of the women when Jesus was captured and crucified, and how wounded they were by the perfidy of Judas and the religious leaders. Would women today be as silent in the face of such monstrous injustice, or would they speak and demonstrate in behalf of the Master?

It is, of course, impossible to analyze all the reasons for people's reprehensible behavior toward their ministers. We are all individuals and do things for different reasons. But in my reflections I can identify three or four of the more prominent, frequently repeated reasons.

One is that some people just naturally have an antipathy toward leaders, whoever they are. The same people openly criticize the president, members of Congress, the governor, the mayor, or anybody in a position of authority. On an analyst's couch, they might be diagnosed as having long-smoldering resentment of the people who held authority over them as children — their parents, their teachers, older siblings, and even class leaders at school. For the remainder of their lives they are compelled to act out their secret hostilities, to vent them on anybody around them who is accepted by others as a leader.

My longtime good friend Dr. Bruce Heilman, who retired from the presidency of the University of Richmond to become its distinguished chancellor, told me that it was a red-letter day in his life as an adminis-trator when he finally realized that the people who were harassing him about anything were not really mad at him personally but were unhappy with the office he represented. The realization occurred one day when a particularly rabid man was admitted to his office while he was president and commenced to flay him for offenses of which he was not really guilty.

"Wait a minute," he thought to himself. "This man is crazy. He thinks I'm responsible for things that occurred before I became president of this institution. I'm not really the target of his animosity, my predecessor is. Maybe it wasn't even my predecessor's fault. This man is simply attacking me because I'm the president of the university. It is the office that is under attack, not me personally."

That insight was invaluable during the rest of his years as an adminis-trator, said Bruce. Whenever anybody came to him virtually foaming at the mouth about a problem, he immediately reminded himself, "Now this isn't personal, it's institutional. This person has a grievance that may not even have a real location, but to him it is very important. I will listen to him and try to defuse his anger. If I cannot, then he will have to carry it away. I'm not going to make it part of my stress today."

Pastors would do well to adopt the same philosophy about all the people who complain to them about what they are doing or not doing and how the church is performing or not performing. Some people are simply possessed by demons of anger and unhappiness with everything. If the minister can exorcise those demons, well and good. But if he or she can't, the people's irritability ought not to be taken to heart and become part of an insuperable burden of dissatisfaction.

Some people are merely pastor-bullies. They expect their ministers to be mild-mannered, good-hearted people motivated by religious devotion to be especially tolerant and accepting of others. Therefore they think they can attack them with impunity, usually satisfying some deep urge to get even with others for all the bullying and abuse they have had to take in their own lives. Psychiatrists say that within the heart of every bully there lurks a defenseless child who has been bullied by someone else. If that is true, then people who like to hector their ministers — and they usually have a reputation for doing it to pastor after pastor — are to be pitied for their own suffering and understood as victims who are trying to avenge themselves.

The bullying is often directed against the weakest member of the pastor's family, not just against the pastor. Often people criticize or belittle the pastor's spouse or child, depending on which one appears the most vulnerable. We have one dear friend who was a pastor's wife for many years. She said that in one pastorate she cried herself to sleep every night for years because of the way certain parishioners treated her and her husband. She had been taught, and indeed counseled by her husband, not to fight back or respond in kind to people, because ministers and their wives were supposed to be examples to others.

I plead guilty to having advised my own wife not to return evil for evil but to turn the other cheek, and I regret now the memories of the way certain people treated her because she appeared to be passive under attack. I remember, for example, how some women belittled her one Sunday in our church narthex where we had set up an angel tree for people to take the names of prisoners' families and prepare Christmas packages for them. Anne had wanted to help with the prisoners' ministry, and this seemed to be a suitable way to do it. She was organizing the gift program and sat at a little desk near the tree to record the names people took and keep track of when the presents came in to the church.

"Next thing we know," one woman remarked snidely to another, careful to say it loudly enough for Anne to hear, "she'll have a tin cup and be selling pencils on the street corner."

When we were at our Los Angeles church, she took the most flak for befriending the many gays in our congregation. One woman, an aggressive, outspoken person who was on the church council and in the chancel choir, took us out to breakfast at a little coastal restaurant shortly after we arrived and lectured Anne on how she should behave toward the gays.

We were eager to make our ministry there a success, so neither of us spoke back to the woman about her attitude. Now we wish we had. I've told earlier, in chapter two, how another prominent woman in the church called and berated Anne for having hugged a man who had AIDS and came to our church seeking help.

Fortunately, Anne is made of pretty strong stuff and didn't always pay attention to our rule that any trouble she got into on Sunday I would have to clean up on Monday and the rest of the week. She spoke back so strongly to one woman that the woman had nothing to do with us for the remainder of our stay in that church. We both regret that we didn't confront people more readily when they came to us with accusations or complaints. It might have landed us in more trouble than we had, but at least there would have been a modicum of satisfaction in doing so.

I have laughed many times at the story of a minister I heard about in North Carolina who responded to a rumor started by two spinster sisters in his church. He had gone downtown for shopping and had parked his car in front of an ABC store. One of the sisters saw it there and told her sibling. Together, they began spreading the word that their minister had a drinking problem. They had seen his vehicle parked outside the liquor store. When the story got back to the minister and he pieced together what had happened, he made an extremely eloquent nonverbal retort: he parked his car in front of the sisters' house, walked away, and left it there overnight!

⌒

Some church members, I am sure, try to hector their ministers because they regard them as servants and therefore inferior to themselves. It is a mentality going all the way back to ancient times and patterns of slavery. If the minister is hired by the congregation, then every church member is in a sense that minister's employer, and therefore his or her superior.

I once met a Methodist minister who said he had a man in his congregation who took every possible occasion to remind the minister that he was somehow inferior to the people who employed him. One day, he said, the man showed up at his front door with a boxful of old potatoes. "Here," said the man, thrusting them at him, "I was pulling the sprouts off the potatoes in my cellar and decided that this bunch was past it. So I thought I might as well give them to you." It was reminiscent of the days, not too far in the past, when people paid their cooks and housemaids in extra bits of food and discarded clothing.

I'll always be convinced that my boyhood pastor, Dr. Preston Ramsey, was virtually killed by a few people in our church who were always putting pressure on him to remind him that he was only a pastor and not the chief authority in the congregation. He was a proud man and never let them bludgeon him into submission. But this probably only added fuel to the fire. In the end, his blood pressure soared through the roof. Forced to submit his resignation, he died before reaching the age of sixty. If he had been in any other line of work, where his career did not depend on the goodwill of those he served, he would have lived at least another twenty years.

I realize that I had an advantage over many of my colleagues in ministry because I had been a professor and had written a lot of books. This tended to command a certain amount of grudging respect from the people who might have used me much more cruelly if it had not been the case. But I still encountered people—mostly men—who thought that their professions in the "real" world of medicine or law or manufacturing granted them an automatic superiority over clergy, giving them the right to bluster and command. If I had been a person of true intelligence, they sometimes implied, I wouldn't have become a minister, I would have done something more sensible with my life.

Even this slight vulnerability, if it could be called that, has made me very sensitive to the plight of many of my fellow ministers who haven't enjoyed my advantages. I think of one friend, for example, whose church board humiliated him when an annual review highlighted the church's terrible economic plight. On the recommendation of a well-to-do board member, the board voted to dismiss both the pastor's secretary and the custodian of the church building, and then told the minister that until things improved it would be necessary for him to mow the lawn and clean the building.

"Here I am," he said, "called to preach the gospel, and what am I doing? I'm cleaning toilets!"

～◌

Although I hate to admit it, I am sure that certain church members appear to behave unkindly toward their ministers because they honestly believe they must act in behalf of their institutions. That is, if they think that their ministers are failing to fulfill their obligations to the churches as preachers, CEOs, or pastoral caregivers, and that the churches are suffering from the fault or neglect of the pastors, they may act in blunt or destructive ways to press the ministers to resign and vacate their posts.

I have mentioned in previous chapters two ministers who were compelled to give up their charges, one because of personal illness and the other because his wife had a stroke and he could no longer manage a large church the way he once did. In both of these cases, I could under-stand the church's position. It didn't matter if those pastors were school principals, business managers, or secretaries. If they were no longer able to meet the requirements of their jobs, then it was necessary for them to step aside so that their churches could employ ministers who were unhampered by their problems.

But it is a different matter when people simply decide that ministers are not performing up to their standards and they begin to persecute the min-isters in various ways to goad them into leaving. I have known ministers whose salaries were reduced, whose workloads were increased, who were the targets of gossip and innuendo, and who were virtually blackmailed into resigning their posts, all because a small group of parishioners became unhappy with them and conspired to force their resignations.

One such minister was doing an excellent job in his church, and had even won an award as pastor of the year from the local association of his denomination. But a small coterie of people in his church resented him because he often preached about Jesus and the poor, and they began to ridicule him as "Brother Bleeding Heart." Soon they were spreading all kinds of rumors and allegations about him, including the suggestion that he might be a child molester. They even complained that he drove a foreign car—a Toyota—and not a "good old American vehicle" such as a Ford or a Chevrolet.

"It all became a game," he told me. "It was called 'Get the Preacher.' One thing led to another, and it all got out of hand. I couldn't do anything right or say anything right. I knew I wouldn't have any peace until I left. So I finally resigned and took another church."

☙

Perhaps it is how churches behave at this critical juncture that determines how Christian they really are. If they are creative and compassionate toward their ministers, displaying real thoughtfulness about the terms of separation and how those terms are administered, they can greatly ameliorate the humiliation and suffering of their pastors during these unfortunate ordeals. If, on the other hand, they are brutish and unfeeling, they can wreak emotional damage and havoc that will torment the ministers all of their lives.

I have heard of cases in which certain church officials not only forced their pastors out but actually followed them vindictively once they had left, besmirching their names and vilifying them in libelous ways. Two of these cases involved Dr. Peter Nost and Dr. William Bradshaw, ministers who served the First Congregational Church of Los Angeles before my time there. Another involved Dr. Herbert Gilmore, an illustrious Baptist pastor and writer.

Dr. Nost was handpicked by Dr. James Fifield to succeed him at the First Congregational Church of Los Angeles. He had been Fifield's favorite associate minister and was, according to all reports I have heard, a sensitive, spiritual man who contrasted in many ways with the active, administratively ingenious Fifield. He had barely entered upon his duties as senior minister of the church when Fifield turned on him and began to undermine his effectiveness. Several of Fifield's loyal friends among the church officers began a campaign to get rid of Nost. Confused and unhappy, Nost had a nervous breakdown and resigned his post. Two decades later, when I was minister of the church, one of the leading laywomen spoke vituperatively of Nost and said that she and other members had pursued him wherever he went and "exposed" him for "who he really was."

The same thing happened to Dr. Bradshaw, who by many reports had enjoyed a very successful seven-year ministry at First Congregational Church. Bradshaw's wife became the minister of education for the church and did a very commendable job of organizing the Sunday school, youth program, and relations with the private school operated by the church. Several of the church's old guard feared that the Bradshaw team was becoming too powerful, so began planning to undercut their work in any way they could. One way they did this was to lobby the congregation to pass a rule removing the minister from direct contact with the nominating committee that produced an annual slate of nominees for all church offices. The minister would have a "representative" of his choosing on the committee, but only in a listening capacity, not as an adviser or active participant.

When Bradshaw was finally forced out of his position, two or three leading laypeople began to actively spread the word that he had been unsatisfactory as their minister and would disappoint any committee that recommended him to another church. As a consequence, Bradshaw returned to the East without employment, and eventually found a job as president of a small, struggling private college in Kentucky. When word leaked back to L.A., he told me, his enemies began immediately phoning and writing trustees and other administrative officers at the college in the attempt to destroy him. Eventually he was able to quell the unrest produced by the church members' vitriolic reports about him, but his situation never became as pleasant and workable as it had been before.

Dr. Herbert Gilmore was minister of a large, prosperous church in Washington, D.C., when he was invited to become pastor of the First Baptist Church of Birmingham, Alabama. He asked about the church's position on integration, as he did not wish to minister to a church that had not accepted the presence of black citizens in its membership. Receiving assurance that the church had recently voted to receive black members, he agreed to the call.

On Gilmore's first Sunday as minister of the Birmingham church, a distinguished local physician came forward and presented herself for membership. She was African American. Gilmore was in the process of presenting her to the congregation and asking its formal approval when one of the deacons came forward, said, "Dr. Gilmore, I think this matter needs a little more time," and indicated that the board of deacons wished to discuss the applicant at a meeting later that week. Stunned, but assuming that this was the strategy adopted by the board to allay any public outbursts, Gilmore assented.

At its meeting, the board waffled on its earlier commitment. Gilmore insisted on adherence to their promise to him. The woman's application for membership was approved, but Gilmore's relationship as pastor was affected and he said that from then on it was "a rocky road, all uphill." Two or three years later, when he was on a trip to Africa, a popular associate pastor undermined him and took control of the church. When he returned and found his own authority as senior minister greatly diminished, he resigned and began the search for another pastorate.

"Everywhere I thought I had secured a position," he later told me, "they found out and fouled my traces." He listed several prominent churches that had been interested in his services. But each time, someone from the First Baptist Church of Birmingham had spread rumors about him or had managed to get an official of the Southern Baptist Sunday School Board in Nashville to do it. "Their networking skills were amazing," said Gilmore. "I couldn't believe it. After the first three or four times, I took extra precautions to keep them from learning about my discussions with pulpit committees. But somehow they found out, and always they stuck the knife in and then the committees said, 'Don't call us, we'll call you.'"

I didn't meet Herb Gilmore until this sad and difficult saga was over. A mutual friend asked me to contact him after he and his wife moved to a log house near Gatlinburg, Tennessee, and she became a schoolteacher to support them. I called him one day to say Anne and I were staying in a Gatlinburg motel and I would like to meet him. We met for coffee at a little restaurant near their house and talked for four hours. Correction, *Gilmore* talked for four hours. His troubled psyche was tamped down and running over with unresolved bitterness over the way he had been treated. He felt that his life and ministry had been ruined by treacherous church members.

Gilmore did occasional interim pastorates in the Gatlinburg area, and eventually, a couple of years before he died, accepted an appointment as pastor of a small United Methodist church at Methodism's minimum salary. His former church members had made a nightmare of his life. I urged him to write a book about his experience—he had already written one about the struggle for racial integration—because I thought it might help him to lay the ghosts of the past. But he was too upset even to do that. He died a broken man, severely punished for his commitment to racial equality in the church.

✧

It is incredible that Christians would dream of treating ministers with this kind of unrelenting viciousness. In the end, I am sure it has something to do with what I talked about in the first chapter, that the church is in many cases a corporate institution and not a collection of spiritual, caring individuals. Those who control the institution, or desire to control it, often exhibit unusual venom and vindictiveness in dealing with the leaders they oppose. Their actions exceed all boundaries of civility and propriety.

I remember a young woman at the School of Theology at Claremont who asked if she could meet with me privately outside of class. I met her in the library and we had coffee and talked for a couple of hours. She was a ministerial student and was serving her internship at a local United Methodist church. There was some ruckus in the church, she said, because a little group of lay people were trying to get the bishop to remove the pastor, but she hadn't paid much attention, figuring that there were probably some political factors she wouldn't understand.

Then, one Saturday night, she realized that she needed her notebook from the church office to finish preparing for a Sunday school class she was going to teach the next morning. So she drove to the church at a little before midnight to get it. When she arrived at the church, she saw lights burning in some of the classrooms and thought that somebody might have broken into the building. So she parked at the side of the parking lot and crept across the lawn to look into a window.

What she saw took her breath away, she said. There were several people whom she recognized hard at work trashing the rooms. They wrote and drew pictures on the blackboards, dumped papers and books on the floors, dusted the chalk erasers on chairs, disarranged the furniture, and generally made a havoc of the place. One of the accusations some members had made against the minister, she told me, was that he wasn't tough enough on the custodial staff. These people were actually destroying the order of the classrooms in order to make the minister look bad in the eyes of all the laypeople who would use those rooms on Sunday!

"I don't know if I can go on to ordination and become a minister," the young woman said. "I never dreamed that church people could be so treacherous and underhanded. I don't think I could cope with something like this in my own church, so maybe it's best if I drop out now."

I tried to help her to absorb what she had seen by reminding her that this was only a small proportion of the membership of that church, and that most of the people were probably kind, gentle folks who supported the pastor. But I had to admit that there are some people in almost every congregation who occasionally behave very badly, and that usually the good guys don't come to the rescue of the person under attack. I don't know if she went on to become a minister. She was so shaken by that experience that she might have decided to become a school teacher or a missionary instead. But it is likely, if she did proceed to the pastorate, that by now she herself has experienced some dust-ups with mean and over-bearing church members.

Sometimes I jokingly say that John Calvin's theology can be summed up in a simple sentence: "People are no damned good!" But there are times when it isn't really a joke. Calvin also talked a lot about the sovereignty of God, and that's important to counterbalance the willfulness of humanity. Yet his estimate of human nature was probably not far off the mark. Some of the best people I know have been capable of some of the most dastardly deeds. That's what imparts an air of betrayal to what they do. We all have a dark side to our personalities, a side we don't even know ourselves. We can't ever say what we would do under certain circumstances. And what happens in churches a lot of times is that people get bent out of shape over something a minister does or says—maybe in conjunction with something else that's happening in their lives, like a bladder infection or the loss of a job—and they say and do things they might not ordinarily do. Later, they may be ashamed of how they acted. But at the time it is all they can do, the only way they can respond. As the Apostle said, sometimes we do the evil we don't want to do and fail to do the good we would really like to do.

I hope that's the way it was with those people in that Methodist church who wanted the bishop to move their pastor. They were behaving miserably. So do a lot of folks in a lot of churches. Does it mean that they don't love God and want to serve him? No, not necessarily. They may not love him as much as they ought to, so that it transforms their way of interacting with others in the world. But when they do love him as they should, they begin to see how they've acted and can feel repentant for their attitudes. The problem is that they don't always live up to their insights and promises. We don't, because we're all guilty in the same way, even if to different degrees. It was a wise person who said we always hurt the ones we love.

◡◠

How should a pastor react under fire? I have a dear friend who almost took his own life because he was having such grief in his church. He was very depressed and went for days without being able to sleep. One morning, when it was barely daylight, he drove headlong into a large statue with his car's speedometer registering sixty miles an hour, intending to kill himself. Fortunately, he survived. But he never pastored another church, for the crash left him physically debilitated.

Sometimes I think that what happened to him was kinder than what often happens to clergy who live on such intimate terms with their ecclesiastical torturers. Their depression takes the form of a slow-dripping torture, of gradually losing all their joy and idealism, and beginning to live in a world of endless torment and betrayal.

When I left my Los Angeles pastorate and became a professor again, I sought the help of a fine psychiatrist to help me recover my enthusiasm for life. She was a Jungian analyst, so she encouraged me to notice my dreams and report them to her. For several weeks, at the beginning of therapy, I recorded bizarre dreams of pursuit and persecution, in which I was trying to escape long, threatening arms that reached out toward me in the darkness of unfamiliar streets, and of having to clean up filth and excrement left behind by others. My analyst was almost dismissive: these are all emblematic of ministers' dreams, she said; all ministers feel threatened, and all must deal with the ordure of their fellow church members. I had escaped, and eventually my dreams became transmogrified into bright, happy experiences. But what of all my friends who didn't make it, the ones who were still slogging along in ministry, having to repress their urges to get out or to retaliate against the perfidy of their parishioners?

I wish a lot of this stuff had been explained to us in seminary—that, even there, we had begun to suspect that the church is what A. O. Taylor, the great medievalist, once called the Roman Catholic church of the Middle Ages, "a spotted reality," and not the pure and adulterated bride of Christ we imagined it was. It would have been helpful to have heard, even if we couldn't believe it then, that there are pathological and treacherous church members waiting in every parish to attack their ministers, sometimes in unbelievably devious ways, and that we must not take it personally, any more than my friend Bruce Heilman did in a university presidency, because they are not after us in particular but after the figure who wears a big red target on his or her back. Surely it is true that being forewarned is to be forearmed. At least it would have minimized the shock and surprise, and we could have said, "Ah, yes, I was warned about this in seminary. It's happening, and I must not take it too much to heart. It is the same kind of reaction that put Jesus on a cross and has afflicted leaders from the beginning of time."

Maybe it is risky to identify what happens to us too much with what happened to Jesus, but it can be a helpful exercise if we don't get to idolizing ourselves overmuch in the process. There are people in the world who are naturally drawn to the truly good persons around them with the intent of doing them in. The evil the Bible speaks of is not a figment of the theological imagination. It actually exists. And, in true Zoroastrian fashion, it actively seeks the destruction of good. It is too idealistic for us to believe that the church, because it is an institution with Jesus as its founder, is immune to evil or does not foster it at its own heart. Evil is everywhere, and often masquerades as goodness or concern or righteousness. Certainly it was masquerading as all these things in the Judaism of Jesus' day, and it was Jesus' relentless attack on this institutional hypocrisy that brought about his death.

Did Jesus really *have* to die for the sins of the world? It is convenient to think that God made him the scapegoat for all of us and that putting a communion wafer in our mouths can exonerate us like a snap of the fingers. It was also a good image for the Jews in the Apostle Paul's synagogue audiences, because they were accustomed to offering sacrifices for their sins and it was an easy transference to claim that Jesus was the super-sacrifice, the once-for-all sin offering for the world. But God himself never needed anything like that to save anybody; he was always in the salvation business, long before the death of Jesus. No, Jesus died because there were evil, insecure people in the world who knew they would feel better if they could get rid of him and no longer have to deal with his needling wit or his insistent way of chipping away at the foundations of their system. They killed him, thinking they would put an end to him and the threat he boded for their existence.

I have a theory—"I could be wrong," as the theme song of the TV show *Monk* says—that the better a minister is, the more likely he or she is to be persecuted by unfriendly elements in the church. Deeply flawed ministers often appear to fare better in the church than their spiritually superior counterparts. More familiar with meanness and evil in their own make-up, they tend to be more combative than ministers who live by the spirit of Christ, and thus to emit the kind of pheromones that warn off their enemies. Some of the greatest charlatans I have known in the ministry have been the least touched by problems in their congregations. They could shift ground in an instant, turn their coats without batting an eye, lie, wheedle, and deceive, and generally outflank their opposition with a skill that would put the CIA to shame. But the good ministers, the ones who were kind, thoughtful, and well-intentioned, almost invariably get hurt by their congregations.

I had dinner recently with a good minister, a man of honor and integrity who has always behaved in the truest way as a man of God, and I asked him what he had endured during forty years of pastorates. His wife uttered a little cry when I asked the question, as if it stabbed her with the pain of a thousand bad memories. He thought for a moment, then said, "Well, I suppose the meanest thing that ever happened was one night when I had been meeting with a man who wanted to run the church and we didn't see eye to eye. When I came out of the church, all four of my tires had nails driven into them." But there was no rancor in his voice, no fierce-ness in his eyes, as he related this. Somehow, in the goodness of his heart and the faith that had sustained him through all those years of ministry, he had managed to transcend such petty acts of vengeance and regard them as part of the human comedy.

That is the way it ought to be, I think, with every servant of God. We see the world—and the church—for what they are, and realize that the fact that some people are church members doesn't make them de facto saints. So when somebody does something particularly noxious or unjust to us, we aren't goaded to return evil for evil. Instead, we shake our heads, remembering that their behavior is simply part of an ageless contest between the good and evil in the world, and decline to lower our own standards to meet theirs. We are, after all, followers of Jesus, who, while he was as tough as nails, counseled turning the other cheek and praying for those who willfully abuse us.

I have always loved a story I read once about a Quaker about to be hanged by two villainous men who stopped him as he drove his wagon along a country road. The men were thrown into sudden fury with one another because neither had remembered to bring along a rope. Calmly reaching into the wagon behind him and lifting a hank of rope, the Quaker said, "It looks as if thee wilt have to use mine."

All ministers need an inner peace that acts as a gyroscope to keep them on an even keel when parishioners are behaving in less than Christian fashion. But it would still have helped if somebody had warned us it was going to be like this.

Seven

The Calling to Be a Minister Transcends All the Problems that Being a Minister Entails

In the end, ministers don't work for their churches, they work for God. The churches always think they work for them, because they provide them with office space and pay their salaries. But such thinking is mistaken, whether it is the churches that think it or the ministers who occupy their office space. If this is not borne in mind, it will lead to all kinds of distortions of the minister's self-image and the church's authority in the total scheme of things.

Part of the confusion stems from the nomenclature we use. We say that God calls a minister, but we also say that a church calls its ministers. In a way, both are true. But the two callings are very different. When God calls a minister—lays a hand on his or her life the way he did on Moses and Jesus and Paul and Augustine—it is a transcendent calling, one that involves lifelong commitments or at least lifelong effects from the momentary realization of a commitment. Only persons who have received such a calling have any idea of how earth-shaking and completely reorienting it can be.

I had always intended, before my calling, to be an artist. I loved to draw and paint, and people said I clearly had a talent for it. As I said earlier,

I wanted to be an illustrator like Norman Rockwell, who was my idol because of his faithful representation of people in extremely human and vulnerable situations. He was a kind of modern-day Brueghel, but with a great sense of humor. But when I finally felt my calling—I had had distant rumblings of it before it struck with irresistible force—it turned my whole life around. Within a few hours of my realization that I would be a minister and not an artist, I had to change my plans and go to a university instead of an art school. I joined my high school's newly formed debate team in order to hone my abilities as a speaker. I realized that I would need a wife who would be compatible with and supportive of my ministry. My father, who was contemptuous of ministers, told me that I could not count on any support from him in getting my education. My calling had spun me around and sent me in an utterly new direction in life.

In my lifetime, I was called by a number of churches to be their pastor. This was a very different sort of calling, and much less far-reaching in its implications. There was a kind of sacredness about it, I hope. I believe that in each instance the church thought it was doing something important and even holy, and I know that I felt some sense of divine leadership in accepting the church's invitation. But not once, in all the callings I had from churches, was I spun around in a new direction. Each time it was only an augmentation of my original calling from God. The church provided a salary and a place where I could spend several years of my life fulfilling my original calling to ministry.

Now, because ministers are called by God in a way that is infinitely higher and more demanding than any call from a human institution known as a church, they should live with a sense of inner authority—from God, not themselves—that puts them spiritually and emotionally beyond the vicissitudes that may occur to them in their callings from particular churches they serve during their lifetimes. Roger Babcock once depicted the person of faith as one who floats like a little duck on the ocean, effortlessly rising and falling with the waves, and never pulled under or destroyed by them. That is an apt image as well for ministers who serve churches. There will always be problems in the churches—even the best of them—because they are still only earthly institutions, regardless of how fine or faithful they may be, and the people who constitute their corps of leaders are frail and inadequate creatures easily led astray by evil. But ministers whose sense of their original callings is strong and vivid in their memories should never permit the problems to submerge them.

Sometimes the evil in a local church is so strong, and the members are so convulsed by it, that it becomes necessary for a minister to leave and locate in another church that is more civil or more hospitable. Ernest Campbell, of New York's Riverside Church, said in a sermon that shaking the dust off our feet, which Jesus advised when certain villages didn't accept the teaching of his Apostles, ought to have been made a sacrament, something accorded the status of a holy necessity. He was right, as he so often was. There comes a time in our dealings with almost any church when it is important to break it off and go. Staying longer would be a disservice to everybody, including God.

I remember saying to a group of ministers when I was preparing to leave my church in Los Angeles that I had never before employed the word "reprobate" but that it was popping up in my head more and more frequently as I considered the experiences I had had with certain people in that church. If I had stayed, I said, I would feel the necessity of having a service of exorcism, and formally attempting to cast the evil from both the building and the congregation. Harry Butman, an elderly minister even then (he lived to be more than a hundred), heard me say that. He had served two or three times in an interim capacity with the church, and the term excited him. Maybe he recognized the applicability of it. But he mentioned it to a couple of strong-headed attorneys in the congregation and they became very angry with me. If anything, they demonstrated the very qualities I was trying to describe by using that ancient legal and ecclesiastical term. In fact, I am sure they wanted to drive me out before I had a chance to perform an assault on their demons.

Some people expostulated that I had a duty to stay with that church, as I had been called to it. But I corrected their thinking by pointing out that my higher calling was to ministry, not to their church in particular, and that, while I believed God had wanted me to come to the church when I came, I now believed that God wanted me to terminate my relationship with it and move on, gathering up the skirts of my calling as I departed.

〜

The minister's calling from God certainly transcends all earthly callings, even the ones that don't come to us. Many ministers' lives, I have found, are profoundly influenced by whether they get invited to certain churches they greatly admire or desire to be pastor of. The larger and more prestigious the church, the more this tends to be true. I just mentioned Ernest Campbell and Riverside Church in New York. I have known at least four excellent, highly competent ministers whose lives were deeply affected by their not being called to be minister of that distinguished church on the Hudson River.

One was a Congregationalist from Boston who fully expected to follow Campbell in that widely known pulpit. I knew about him because his brother, also a minister, was presently taking a course with me at Vanderbilt Divinity School and one day he accompanied his brother to the class. In introducing him, the brother announced that our guest, his brother, would be the next minister at Riverside. I raised my eyebrow at the news, for I had myself had overtures from the search committee, which I did not treat very seriously, and had heard nothing of this brother. A few weeks later, the church announced that it had invited the Rev. William Sloane Coffin, chaplain at Yale University, to be their next minister.

A few years later, I was preaching in the Boston minister's church, only now he was in Seattle, Washington, whence he had relocated because he had become so discontent with his life in Boston. We talked about the

Riverside business, and he admitted that a woman on the search committee had confided to him that she expected him to be their choice.
Later, he said, the woman had moved to Boston and joined his church.
When she did, she told him in a very candid conversation that Coffin had
been a shoe-in from the beginning, but that the committee had been at
pains to conduct a nationwide search and make it appear as if they were
really talking with many people before making their decision. Failing to
go to Riverside, the pastor said, had been an enormous disappointment to
him — so much so that he became extremely frustrated and even considered leaving the ministry altogether. The Seattle church had caught him
on his emotional rebound.

Another candidate who was taken in by the very same ruse and during
the very same pastoral search happened to be a bishop in the United
Methodist Church. He too had been convinced that he would be the
next minister at Riverside and had announced as much to many friends.
He was so unhappy after he discovered that he had been misled by the
committee that he renounced his bishopric and moved to Denver, where
for several years he became a seminary teacher and then gradually faded
from visibility.

A third minister who was fully expecting to be called to Riverside,
again during the same search period, was pastor of a large, well-known
congregation in Columbus, Ohio, and the son of a bishop. He became so
agitated when he didn't get the New York appointment that he resigned
his post in Columbus, divorced his wife, and eventually opened a retreat
center in New York State. He remarried, wrote a very honest book about
his disillusionment, and for several years had a fairly eventful life as director
of the center, which tended to attract disenchanted ministers as a major
part of its clientele.

The fourth pastor I knew who was crestfallen over not being called to
Riverside Church was a fellow pastor, a United Methodist, whose church
was near my own in Los Angeles. He told me confidentially that he
was expecting the call any day — this was after William Sloane Coffin

retired—because members of the church's search committee had been to hear him several times and had assured him that he was their choice. I tried, as a friend, to warn him not to set his expectations too high. I told him about the disappointed suitors the last time around, when Coffin had been called. But he was so confident of being the new minister at Riverside that he sent his daughter off to college in New York so where they would be able to see each other frequently.

I had been to New York several times to preach at Riverside and other churches, and I told my friend that I believed it was time for Riverside to call an African-American pastor, as the congregation there was becoming increasingly black in its makeup. I knew the Rev. Dr. James Forbes, the African-American professor of preaching at Union Theological Seminary in New York, and understood that he was popular as a supply preacher at Riverside. I could be wrong, I told my friend, but if I were a betting man I would put my money on Forbes to succeed Coffin. And, sure enough, Forbes did become the next minister of Riverside.

My friend was beside himself in anger and disappointment. He felt that the committee had toyed with him. "They played me for a fool!" he exclaimed one day as we were driving to a ministers' conference at Dana Point, several miles south of Los Angeles. "What will you do now?" I asked him. "I can't stay here," he said. "I've mentally packed and moved back East. My daughter's in school there. I've got to follow."

Several weeks later, I learned that he and his wife were getting a divorce and he was moving to Concord, Massachusetts, where he had taken a position with a large consulting firm.

How many other ministers, I wonder, had their lives disrupted by their failure to be called as minister of that big church on the Hudson? The number, I'm sure, is diminutive in comparison with the number of ministers who receive similar disappointments from other churches across the United States. I hear every two or three weeks from some minister—often one of my former students—who tells a familiar story about being dejected at not being chosen for a post he or she was bent upon having.

"The grass is always greener," as they say, and many ministers live in constant hope of a bigger, better, or more prestigious appointment.

I have had my share of disappointments too. But one thing I learned a long time ago is that many of the churches that ministers desire so fervently are not nearly so attractive from the inside as they appear from the outside. I have known pastor after pastor who telephoned in triumph to announce that they were leaving their old churches for new ones, only to call a few months later and spend an hour lamenting that they had succumbed to the glamor of the new places and wishing they were back at their former posts. So I have managed, in spite of the disappointments, to sail along like that little duck, content with my calling from God even when my lesser calling from a particular church was nothing to brag about.

I greatly admire the few ministers I know who have never been tempted by the blandishments of bigger and wealthier congregations, or congregations in more interesting places, or congregations that might have made them feel better for a time by paying more attention to them or ensconcing them in more attractive surroundings. There aren't many of them, but they are the salt of the earth. They appear to know, almost instinctively, that God has more work for them to do where they are, so their antennae are never out to detect the vibrations of vacant pulpits or newly mobilized search committees.

I think of my friend Nathan Brooks, a Baptist minister in Lynchburg, Virginia, who was pastor of Peakland Baptist Church for more than twenty years. The church had a lot of ups and downs during those years, and I often heard a rumor that Nathan was battling for his life or was actually leaving. But in the end, the upheavals would settle down and Nathan would still be there, chugging along like the good, responsible pastor he was and ignoring the possibility of finding another church where folks might appreciate him more.

He reminded me of a story I read once in The *Atlantic* about a little burro that had become a fixture on a certain western ranch. The ranch hands liked to tell the burro's story, for it was heroic in its way. One day, they said, there was a steer on the ranch that nobody could tame. So out of desperation, they leashed it with a rope to the little burro and turned the two animals loose. The steer struck out for distant places, yanking at the burro's line and sometimes even tossing it over its back. They were gone for several days. Then, one day, someone gave a call and everybody came out to watch. The two animals were back, only now the little burro was trotting along home and the steer was following meekly in its wake. From then on, every recalcitrant steer got tied to that burro, and, every time, the burro stayed with it until it was ready to come back and behave itself.

I saw Nathan recently when I was back in Lynchburg to preach at the First Christian Church. He and his wife, Brenda, are singing in the choir at that church. He has been retired for several years and is continuing to offer pastoral counseling out of an office at the Christian church. Like the burro, he is still going. As far as I know, he never met a steer he couldn't tame.

One reason I have done a lot of thinking about the minister's calling vis-à-vis the church's calling is that I have a son, Eric, who was ordained to the ministry in 1987 and is no longer serving a church. When he finished seminary, Eric came on my staff in L.A. as minister of evangelism and pastoral care. Then he became a solo pastor at Avondale Presbyterian Church in Birmingham, Alabama, and a few years later moved from there to the Hogansville Presbyterian Church in suburban Atlanta. I don't think I am merely bragging when I say that he was a very special kind of minister—a thoughtful, creative preacher, a concerned pastor, and a hard-working administrator. He prayed the most searching, poetic prayers I ever heard from a pulpit. In fact, there was something poetic—even *mytho*poetic—about his whole ministry. It was as if he wanted to reinvent ministry at a new and higher level.

His life in ministry, however, was not an easy one. Like his dad, he was an introvert, and an extrovertish career was difficult for him. He loved writing prayers and sermons, and enjoyed delivering them. He liked envisioning church programs and working out the details of them. He even relished visiting church members, especially the elderly, and often sat for hours in a retirement home playing checkers or chess with the residents. But making small talk with average church members drained him, and meeting with boards and committees often left him blitzed for hours afterward. He was a sitting target for mean-spirited church members, especially those in official capacities of any kind, because he was combat-avoidant and could never defend himself in a clutch.

He made three unfortunate marriages, one for each of the churches. This was against him too, even though the search committees in his second and third churches said their congregations weren't judgmental and his experiences would only make him more understanding of their problems. Divorce was OK until some other problem came up. Then it was inevitably a weakness in his armor. His third wife was an attorney for the government. He took his Atlanta church when she was assigned to an office there, and later followed her to Tampa when she became head of an office in that city. But the only churches at which he had a shot in the Tampa area were theologically incompatible for him so he earned his living for a while as a writer for sermon magazines. Then the expectation of those magazines became too pointedly conservative for him.

So four years ago he elected to "transcend" the local church by going back to school for a Ph.D. in depth psychology—which is undoubtedly the most religious kind of psychology because it embraces all theological, philosophical, and mythological traditions—and redirecting his life as a minister without a church. He has not repudiated his ordination or even his intention of being a minister. Instead, he is working on a thesis about ministers who outgrow their church experience and must find satisfying avenues of ministry in other endeavors. As part of his research for the thesis, he is interviewing six former ministers who are no longer serving local churches because, for varying reasons, they have found pastoral work to be tedious, distasteful, or otherwise unsuitable for them.

The controlling mythological image of his research is that of Orpheus, the classical orphan who must make his own way in the world. Ministers who no longer fit the pattern required by churches, he says, are essentially orphaned by the church, so that they are on their own to fulfill their ordination vows. Some do this by becoming counselors in the secular world. Some do it by becoming writers or editors. Others do it by becoming teachers. And still others become insurance salesmen, stockbrokers, hospice attendants, or social workers. The point is, they do not leave ministry because they are no longer pastors. They still have a strong sense of their ordination, or being set aside for the work of God in the world. But finding themselves mismatched with parishes, they search for fulfillment in other ways. They do not regard themselves as failures. On the contrary, some of them regard their friends who did not leave parish work as failures because they have contented themselves with salaried employment that no longer satisfies or challenges the deepest and best they have to offer.

As Eric and I have discussed his research and ruminations on his dissertation topic, I have been compelled to think more deeply about calling than I ever did in my life. I see that in my own case I moved in and out of local ministry, shifting from divinity-school teaching to ministry and eventually back again, without any sense of diminished calling when I was not in a church. Even now, in retirement, I feel a definite sense of ministry in my writing. I have been a minister all along, but with different venues of service. The strength of the call has never faded or become diluted. It has grown even stronger through the years because of the variety of things I have been able to do.

I am convinced—and Eric's research has helped me to work my way through to such a conviction—that being a minister of God is in no way tied to being the pastor of a church. The pastorate is one avenue of ministry, but there are countless others. A minister in the local church ought to know this and feel liberated by the knowledge to consider the possibility of moving away from the church if he or she finds it spiritually stultifying or unrewarding as a life experience. We are not automata who can be made to work acceptably as interchangeable ministers in an ecclesiastical system that is itself in turmoil and transition. Some of us will find the local church a good place to be because it permits us to serve God and people in ways that are agreeable to our natures and our training. But others may well discover that dealing with the local church has a dampening effect on our souls that would be spiritually fatal were we to continue in it for long.

☙

Of all the church orphans I have known, one of the finest, I think, is Joseph Girzone, the author of the famous Joshua novels. Few people know that Joe is a priest who "transcended" the church. A faithful parish priest for many years, and a well-known mediator in New York prison riots, Joe developed heart trouble. When he was fifty, his cardiologist told him that he had to retire or he would probably suffer a massive coronary. When Joe went to his superior and asked to retire, however, his superior, faced with an acute shortage of priests, denied his request. Tired of church bureaucracy, Joe retired without benefits. It was the only way he could leave. For several years, he nearly starved to death. At one time, he was buying frozen dinners, cutting them into thirds, and eating one third at each meal.

The one thing that brought him a little income was the occasional speaking he did for church and secular groups about his experience in the Attica prison riot. But as he continued to drive about for these engagements, he kept thinking about Jesus and what Jesus would have been like if he had lived in contemporary New York State—particularly in Altamont, where Joe lived. Eventually he wrote a book about this modern Jesus, and called him Joshua, the Hebrew name for Jesus. He went to a local printer and told the printer he had a book but no money. The printer agreed to publish the book for two thousand dollars and let Joe pay him when he could. Soon Joe was carrying a couple of boxes of Joshua books with him wherever he went and selling them after his talks.

People who read the simple, unaffected tale of this modern Jesus, a likeable carpenter who came into town and began changing people's lives, told their friends, who told their friends, and so on. Before he knew it, Joe was doing a thriving business in his self-published books. Then a Jewish literary agent read a copy of the book and asked to represent it. He got an offer from a publishing firm of $25,000 for the rights to publish *Joshua*. It was less than he was making each year as his own publisher, but he was tired of handling all those books, so he accepted the offer. The rest is publishing history. Soon more than a million copies of *Joshua* were in print.

Joe went on to write sequels to the original—*Joshua and the Children, Joshua in the Holy Land, Joshua in the City,* and *The Shepherd,* plus a spiritual autobiography called *Never Alone,* a book about the Trinity, one about Mary, Jesus' mother, and several other books.

We were visiting Joe in his hilltop home overlooking the little town of Altamont and his old seminary—there is irony in the fact that the famous author now looks down on the seminary and the office of the superior who cut off his benefits—when he received an advance check in the amount of $175,000 for one of his books. Within thirty minutes, he was on the telephone to a group of nuns in California who needed a new chapel, pledging the entire amount to help them get started. He has been the soul of generosity to many people. He has traveled all over America speaking in churches, schools, and seminaries. There is a Joshua Foundation that extends his work into all the world. And his books continue to sell in the millions, their simple, uncomplicated picture of Jesus blessing the lives of people everywhere.

Joe has never thought of himself as leaving the ministry. He still serves Mass every morning—on the front porch of his home when weather permits. He speaks as a man ordained to the priesthood. But he is no longer hampered by the strictures placed on local priests. His books are frequently critical of the Roman Catholic Church, and have been banned at the Vatican. Yet his ministry grows and grows. People are blessed by his gift for retelling the story of Jesus in straightforward, unadorned prose. They call and write from all over the world. They often travel to Altamont to attend his seminars at the Joshua Foundation. He still has heart problems and has to be careful about his exertions. But I don't know of anyone who has had a more powerful, effective ministry.

⌇

What I would like for ministers to hear is that their calling is from God and not from the church, and therefore God will bless their work whether it is done in the church or out of it. Some will be able to work effectively within the institution of the church, helping Christians to deepen their spiritual lives, to learn more about Christ and his teachings, to minister to others, and to organize themselves for worship and service. But those who cannot do this are not failures because they can't. God didn't make a mistake by calling them into the ministry. He will simply give them something else to do—something where they can continue to serve him in nonpriestly ways.

I talked a few years ago with a young minister who had left the church to become a stock broker. But he had not left the ministry. He simply found that he could not tolerate the critical nature of many of the people he met in the church and preferred to work outside the church.

"What I have seen," he told me, "is that people's finances are very close to their hearts, which means that they are also connected to their sense of spirituality. Everyday I talk with people all over the country about their financial portfolios. As I discuss with them what they want to achieve with their investments, I find that many of them tell me things about their families and what is happening in their lives. They tell me much more as a broker than they ever did when I was a minister. So I am able to talk with them very confidentially and intimately about the things that are either bothering or encouraging them. I don't feel that I have left the ministry. I have merely found my niche."

⌇

I have been saying in this book some of the things I wasn't told about in seminary—that most churches are mere institutions, not true spiritual enclaves; that in the eyes of many church members appearances are considerably more important than reality; that pastoral search committees rarely know or tell the truth about their own organizations, so that ministers seldom realize what they are getting into in a particular church; that every minister is nearly asphyxiated by all there is to do in the average parish; that there are some people in every church who target the minister with all their anger and resentments; and that there are at any given time vast trends in biblical and theological understanding sweeping the country, so that ministers are often drawn unconsciously into modes of interpreting the faith that don't really represent their own thinking or intuition.

Now I am saying that the minister's calling from God somehow trumps all these problems that ministers encounter when they attempt to pastor a local church—not just by allowing them to escape into other forms of ministry but *by permitting them to transcend the very problems that vex and discourage them as they attempt to work in the church.*

What did the Apostle say? "If God is for us, who can be against us" (Romans 8:31). Of course the problems are daunting. Many of us didn't expect them in the church. We thought the church would be better than that—that people would be loving and caring and forgiving, that differences of opinion would be negotiated at the altar, that it would all be a perpetual foretaste of heaven. We are disappointed that it isn't this way, that people in the church can be just as blind and prejudiced and difficult as people in politics or business or any other sphere of life. But hey, what difference does it make, once we've gotten past our illusions and see things as they really are? It would be easy to walk away like spoiled children who don't like the way the game is going—to take our few marbles and go somewhere to play by ourselves. Sticking it out—turning things around, making lemonade out of the lemons—may be God's calling to some of us. And if it's what God wants, who are we to argue?

Having God on our side is the best defense we have as ministers. So the church has become a mere institution? It is a place to start witnessing to the vibrant kingdom. So appearances are more important than reality? Reality needs some help here. So the situation isn't what we were told it would be? Lots of room for improvement. So the minister is overworked? Good place to set priorities and show church members how to order their lives as well. Mean people? The world is full of them. Trends in biblical and theological understanding? Start some new ones!

Most ministers begin their work in the church with a huge set of illusions about what church is, who the members are, and how things operate. Sure, the seminary let us down. Nobody really warned us about how it would actually be. But, once we have got rid of our illusions, we can get down to work. Maybe this is precisely what we were called to do, to come into an impossible situation and begin to change it, to analyze it and face it and scold it and finesse it until we have got it going in another direction. It's possible that it won't ever resemble the church of our dreams. But that's what they were, weren't they, our *dreams*. This is the way the world is. It's the way the church is. Stop complaining. Suck it in and go to work!

It's easy to whine and grouse about not knowing what we were getting into. God knows, I've done enough of that myself. But in the end, when we've spent our years in a lover's quarrel with the church, and have the scars and scratches to prove it, it is the *difference* we made that pleases us most. Not the parties we went to or the epiphanies we felt in worship or the times the congregations remembered our anniversaries and said nice things about our ministries. But the difference we made in the way people behaved inside the institutional framework, or the difference we made in the church's commitment to Christ, or the difference we made in the way certain people came to view the church's mission in the world, or the difference we effected in their daily lives and personal journeys.

These differences aren't set in stone. They're more like the little houses and castles children build from sand on the beach, and they soon get swept away in a new pastorate or a new decade or a new national trend. But they aren't lost in the memory of God, or even in our own memories. The images of them are still there, part of the record of the ages, part of the *story* in history. They keep returning to our minds, and probably to the minds of others, like slides we watched a few minutes ago, and who is to say that they won't influence the future in some more or less permanent ways?

Picasso once said that he didn't mind painting out a color because if it was any good it would come back. Perhaps the same is true of the differences we make. The good ones won't ever disappear for good.

Few things make me happier, now that I've retired, than to receive a letter from someone in one of my parishes that says, "This thought you voiced on such-and-such an occasion changed my life," or to return to the community where I labored and have people remark, "I've never forgotten this-or-that worship service when you were here," or to read a bulletin from one of my old churches and see that they're still using a particular program I helped put into place while I was there. Probably none of these people said anything to me while I was their pastor. We were all too busily caught up in the affairs of the day and trying not to get buried alive by them to notice things with any particular clarity then. But now, looking back, we can see the things that became important as the days went by, and can measure the effectiveness of ministry by that.

I'm still having my lover's quarrel. I'm sure I always will. I heard Stetson Kennedy, the great civil rights activist, talking on Public Radio International the other day. "I want my last breath to be the most militant of all," he said. I expect that's the way it will be with me as well.

There is still so much to be done! But that's why God will go on calling ministers, and why they have to keep throwing themselves into the breach in spite of "the spotted reality" of the church.

Maybe that's why they didn't tell me in seminary. They didn't want me to resign my calling before I'd had a chance to find out for myself.

I've saved the most intimate bit for last. It's about one reason we are unhappy with the problems we discover in the church—because they threaten us. Most ministers I know did not find the church a threatening place when they were growing up. On the contrary, it was a comforting place—a place where people loved us and approved of us. So we got to thinking it would be a good place to live and work for the rest of our lives. Then, when we became ministers and people looked at us as adults and not children, everything seemed different. The church became a scene of conflict and hostility.

We don't like to have our motives and opinions challenged. It undermines our self-esteem. It makes us feel weak and error-prone. We wonder how we could be so bad, why we can't make things work more smoothly.

Well, good news! This is a common problem. A lot of ministers suffer from the same sense of vulnerability.

Even Henri Nouwen, often considered one of the two or three greatest spiritual figures of the twentieth century, was afflicted by it. In *Sabbatical Journey*, the diary of the final year of his life, he wrote about his joy at being back at Daybreak, the community of mentally challenged people near Toronto, Canada, where he served as a chaplain, because he felt accepted there:

> These days I feel strong, alive, and full of energy. Still, I am aware that much of that well-being is the direct result of the loving support of many friends. At the moment I do not experience any anger or hostility directed toward me. I feel in gentle harmony with my family, the people in Daybreak, especially Nathan and Sue, and the many friends close by and far away. In situations like this I easily forget how fragile I am inside, and how little is needed to throw me off balance. A small rejection, a slight criticism might be enough to make me doubt my self-worth and even lose my self-confidence.[5]

How many pastors that could describe! When they are among friends, they feel relaxed, happy, and accepted. Their thoughts are pleasant, they have energy, they feel inspired. But when people speak ill of them, or attack them directly, their self-confidence shrivels and they want to bolt, to get away to an easier life, to have the church of their dreams instead of the one they're stuck with.

Maybe it would help to know how Nouwen coped with his own feelings of self-doubt and inadequacy. He talked about it in the same diary. His defense, he said, was "a spirituality of weakness." It was something he learned from a man named Adam Arnett, who introduced him to the Daybreak community. Adam had severe epilepsy. Yet, despite his disabilities, he had ministered to hundreds of assistants, visitors, and friends at Daybreak. He was Nouwen's friend, and the two of them lived together as housemates. Adam, he said, "reached into the depths of my heart" and "touched my life beyond words." Watching Adam's way with people, and seeing him overcome his personal limitations, had taught Nouwen that it is possible to develop one's spirituality precisely out of the center of one's vulnerability. When Adam died, he spoke of his "incredible spiritual strength."

Is this tantalizing, or isn't it?

The church isn't what we want it to be, and we are more or less powerless to change it. However well-meaning and competent we are, we will never be good enough for the job we've been given to do. The tide of human events is against us. People — adult people, at least — are basically incorrigible. At best, we will touch a few dozen or a few hundred lives in memorable ways. Most of our efforts fall in the same category with trying to drive the flies away from the food at a picnic or rake up the autumn leaves in the forest. We are small, we are weak, we are bound to fail. As the Apostle said, "We have this treasure"— this immense, incredible treasure of the gospel —"in crackable pottery" (2 Corinthians 4:7). We leak, we break, we are basically insufficient for the task.

BUT—I put the word in capitals because it is a huge exception—we are not alone. We are not doing it for ourselves. Our worth will not be judged or validated in eternity by whether we succeed. It is God's Spirit that gives it all its meaning, its value, its justification. We do what we do in his Spirit, not in our own power. We don't have to change the world. That isn't our task, it is God's. We are only the sentinels on guard duty, or the cooks in the mess hall. God is the one who will win the war against evil and meaninglessness. All we have to do is show up, tend our own little gardens, give everything our best shot.

Our real spirituality, like Nouwen's, isn't derived from our success as pastors. It arises straight out of our weakness, our inability to do what we think we ought to be doing, our worried concern for God's world and our role in it. God has rarely used big, important, successful people—kings, queens, emperors, celebrities—to do his bidding. But he frequently uses little, clumsy, insignificant folk—preachers, teachers, social workers, ordinary people and children—to do it.

Of course it's no wonder that we are disappointed when we discover that the church doesn't work the way we thought it would and that we get disgusted when our congregations put their concern for the appearance of things a country mile beyond caring about the reality of them. And it blows us away that our lives as pastors are so filled with apparently trifling, worthless duties, and that some of the people we work with in our churches are meaner than Ebenezer Scrooge before his conversion. But the bottom line isn't about how things really are in the arena where we work, it's about how faithfully we acquit ourselves, how dependable we are in a crunch, how sensitively we are walking and living with God in the midst of this incredible circus that has grown out of Jesus' simple response to Peter's declaration that he was indeed the Son of God, "This is the rock on which I'll establish my church" (Matthew 16:18).

Plato was right—everything in this world is only an imperfect shadow of something that is much better in the world of dreams and ideas. The church is a flawed wonder. It is a miracle that it hasn't already died of its own fumbling inadequacy. But it is a shadow of something flawless and magnificent in the mind of God. And we ministers are only shadows too.

In a perfect world, we would be elbowed out of the way to make room for much finer pastors, much more eloquent preachers, and much better administrators.

But thank God for what we have! It is by his grace that we're given the minor roles we play in this drama of centuries.

Like Nouwen, let's be grateful for "a spirituality of weakness." It is exactly the kind of spirituality Jesus had when he died on a cross. It wasn't the highly symbolic donkey on which he rode into Jerusalem that counted, it was the barrenness of the cross on which he rode out. Our situations may be terrible—like John Bunyan in prison—but we can turn them inside out. It is a privilege to face our impossible situations for Christ!

Notes

1. New York: Doubleday, 1962, p. 236
2. Pp. 175-176
3. January/February 2005, p. 154
4. NY: Doubleday Image Books, 1954, p. 110
5. NY: Crossroad Publishing Co., 1998, p. 131

Acknowledgments

I gratefully acknowledge the loving support of many people in the seven churches I pastored – Bronston Baptist Church in Bronston, Kentucky; Poplar Grove Baptist Church in Rockcastle County, Kentucky; Martin's Pond Union Baptist Church in North Reading, Massachusetts; Raritan Valley Baptist Church in Metuchen, New Jersey; First Presbyterian Church in Lynchburg, Virginia; First Congregational Church of Los Angeles, California; and the Little Stone Church on Mackinac Island, Michigan – and want you to know that you are all still very special to Anne and me, regardless of anything I may have said in this book about the church as an institution that sometimes turns out to be more frustrating than rewarding.

You not only made our ministry bearable, you made it something to celebrate. Your kindness and generosity, then and ever since, have been very important to us. I can easily say, with the Apostle Paul in his Letter to the Philippians, "I thank my God every time I remember you."

And, believe me, we remember you often!

About the Author

John Killinger has had a distinguished career as a churchman, professor, and author. Holder of a Ph.D. in theology from Princeton University and another Ph.D. in literature from the University of Kentucky, he taught preaching, worship, and literature at Vanderbilt Divinity School from 1965 to 1980. He has also taught as a visiting professor at the University of Chicago, City College of New York, Princeton Seminary, and Claremont School of Theology, and was Distinguished Professor of Religion and Culture at Samford University in Birmingham, Alabama.

Ordained as a Baptist minister at the age of eighteen, he left teaching for a decade in the 1980s to be senior minister of the First Presbyterian Church in Lynchburg, Virginia. He then became senior minister of the First Congregational Church of Los Angeles, the oldest English – speaking congregation in that city. Since leaving Samford University in 1996 he has also served as minister of the Little Stone Church on Mackinac Island, Michigan.

Dr. Killinger has written more than fifty books, on subjects ranging from Hemingway and the Theater of the Absurd to prayers, preaching, and biblical commentary as well as fiction. He has also served on the editorial boards of *Christian Ministry, Pulpit Digest* and the Library of Distinctive Sermons.

John and his wife, Anne (also an author), love reading, writing, travel, theater, and hiking. Their rambling home is on the outskirts of Warrenton, Virginia, halfway between the nation's capital and the Blue Ridge Mountains.

A Word from the Editor

A few of these seven important truths I learned the hard way. The rest I never learned at all because, to put it bluntly, I found I did not have the courage nor inclination to continue in the pastoral ministry. On my good days I can clearly state that I did not feel called to pastoral ministry and I did feel called to Christian book publishing. On my days of questioning and doubt I wonder if I really didn't have the stomach for facing these realities head on and seeing what would become of me?

But I certainly had a few amazing mentors who tried to let me know that becoming a minister was one of the most demanding challenges and callings that any man or woman could respond to. One was the Rev. Dr. Homer Goddard, a Presbyterian minister in Richland, Washington whose ministry led to my initial encounter with the living Christ while a freshman at Whitman College. Homer eventually became the first director of extension education at Fuller Theological Seminary in Pasadena, California. I credit his leadership and wisdom for building a division of extension education at Fuller which continues to thrive today. Although, as in most seminary settings, the adjunct professors and extension students are not treated with the honor and respect they are due. But Homer, and subsequent directors and staff, have had the intelligence and grace to navigate the complicated dynamics that often seem to exist between central campus faculties and extension programs. He modeled wise pastoral leadership in a way that was an inspiration to me.

Then there was the Rev. Fred Schultz, a Presbyterian minister, who led the congregation at Canterbury United Presbyterian Church in the San Fernando Valley. He lovingly pushed me to step up into adult ministry tasks, including preaching, in my early twenties and opened my eyes to the challenges of day to day parish ministry in ways that were a revelation to me. Fred had the grace and vision to see that humor can go a long way in the ministry. Humor was not on my list of class options at Fuller.

And finally there was the Rev. Robert Munger, another Presbyterian minister, who came to Fuller Seminary to teach on evangelism and congregational life after many years in successful pastoral ministry. His vision led to the formation of the Faith Renewal Team. These student led teams spent weekends helping churches begin to understand the value of small group ministries. I credit the FRT with actually saving my life. When friends invited me to join the team I was in a very low and discouraged time. If it had not been for the unconditional loving embrace of that group of people and the leadership of Dr. Munger I might never have found my way back to the church nor even to my seminary educa-tion (I had dropped out of seminary a year or so before) and my true calling to religious publishing. Dr. Munger's impact on campus with students was far greater than many faculty or staff even imagined and I will always be grateful for his courage and vision and personal attention during those years of the early 1970s.

So I, along with many other seminarians, went through my theological education not learning these important lessons but fortunately I was able to embrace my education for what it was worth at the time and it has served me well. So I must echo what John has said in his dedication. The professors with only academic backgrounds just didn't know better, although there were others who tried to caution us and train us appropria-tely because they had served in churches.

There are few men or women who would even attempt to write a book such as this one. Courage and independence are often not qualities that the church values and over the past few years as I have worked with John (this is our third book together) I have seen him express that courage and independence in ways that surprise me. And I work and live in a business where it is not easy to surprise me anymore.

What I pray for most is that seminarians will find this book by whatever means and heed its admonitions and as a result, find a way to live out their parish ministries with the same courage and independence that the Reverend Dr. John Killinger lived out his.

Appendix
The Ten Commandments for a Truly Successful Ministry

1. Thou shalt love the Lord thy God with all thy heart and all thy mind and all thy soul, and not worry about whether thy church regards thee with anything like the same degree of passion.

2. Thou shalt have no other gods before God—not even the god of thine own understanding or thine own theology.

3. Thou shalt love thy neighbors—even thy church members—with a love that surpasses the love they show unto thee, and ask God to forgive them for doing many things to thee that they honestly know not.

4. Thou shalt tend to thy knitting as a pastor even when thy needles are dull, thy knitting yarn breaks, and thy light fails. Thou hast assumed an obligation, and thou must fulfill it.

5. Thou shalt work at thy preaching with all thy heart and all thy might and all thy carefully stored notes, for the world still needs to hear that God is there and cares for us—heartbreakingly so.

6. Thou shalt remember to pray for thine enemies with a diligence as great as their antipathy, for they too are sheep in God's pasture, however black and unattractive they may appear to thee.

7. Thou shalt laugh every day at the comedy of the world, including the fact that thou art a pastor and thy church is a bummer. Who knowest when anything funnier will come down the road?

8. Thou shalt visit the sick and the shut-ins as faithfully as thou visitest the bank or the grocery store, and bring them sunshine and roses whenever thou dost, for their lives are often lacking in these.

9. Thou shalt remember to care for thyself along with thy flock, taking thy days off to be with thy family, playing golf if it pleasureth thee, and eating and sleeping healthily, for while thou mayest not be a national treasure, thou art a treasure unto thyself and thy loved ones, and worthy of the the most infinite care.

10. Thou shalt live thankfully from the rising of the sun to the going down of the same, for thy life is amongst the most favored in the world, and few there be who are so richly blessed. The Lord loveth a cheerful giver, and thou art supposed to be giving thy ministry the best that is within thee. So put thou a smile on it!

Of Related Interest

WINTER SOULSTICE
Celebrating the Spirituality of the Wisdom Years
John Killinger

John Killinger has long been a trusted voice and elder statesman for mainstream American Christians. In this extended meditation, Dr. Killinger shows how age gives us a richer understanding of the different aspects of our lives — memories, ambitions, work, conflicts, and even sex. True spiritual growth occurs when we see our memories and experiences, our choices and failures to choose, our friendships and associations, come together like the streams of a river to form the spiritual beings we have become.

0-8245-2316-4, $19.95 paperback

crossroad

Of Related Interest

John Killinger
TEN THINGS I LEARNED WRONG
FROM A CONSERVATIVE CHURCH

In this eloquent memoir, John Killinger, one of the grand figures of conservative Protestantism, reveals what he learned from his upbringing and how, with trust in God and compassion for others, his faith matured. With gentle humor and compassion, Killinger shows us how faith is a constant, even as our beliefs and the world around us change. This story will be of help to many who wish to remain faithful to the Lord, but struggle with the strict tenets of biblical fundamentalism.

0-8245-2011-4, $19.95 paperback

crossroad